DATE DUE   FEB   2007

ARNOLD SCHWARZENEGGER
From Superstar to Governor

Sally Lee

Enslow Publishers, Inc.
40 Industrial Road
Box 398
Berkeley Heights, NJ 07922
USA
http://www.enslow.com

Library of Congress Cataloging-in-Publication Data

Lee, Sally.
    Arnold Schwarzenegger : from superstar to governor / Sally Lee.
      p. cm. — (People to know today)
    Includes bibliographical references and index.
    ISBN-10: 0-7660-2625-6—ISBN-13: 978-0-7660-2625-6 (hardcover)
    1. Schwarzenegger, Arnold—Juvenile literature. 2. Governors—California—
Biography—Juvenile literature. 3. California—Politics and government—1951—Juvenile
literature. 4. Bodybuilders—United States—Biography—Juvenile literature. 5. Actors—
United States—Biography—Juvenile literature. I. Title. II. Series.
F866.4.S38L44 2006
979.4'054'092—dc22
                            2005020399

Printed in the United States of America

10 9 8 7 6 5 4 3 2 1

To Our Readers: We have done our best to make sure all Internet Addresses in this book were
active and appropriate when we went to press. However, the author and the publisher have no
control over and assume no liability for the material available on those Internet sites or on
other Web sites they may link to. Any comments or suggestions can be sent by e-mail to
comments@enslow.com or to the address on the back cover.

Every effort has been made to locate all copyright holders of material used in this book. If any
errors or omissions have occurred, corrections will be made in future editions of this book.

Illustration Credits: Artville, LLC, p. 14; AP/Wide World, pp. 1, 4, 7, 44, 48, 50,
54, 61, 62, 66, 72, 74, 76, 80, 82, 84, 87, 93, 95, 97, 101, 102, 106, 108, 110,
113; Michael Montfort / Shooting Star, pp. 15, 16, 24, 30, 36, 56;
©JupiterImages Corporation, p. 26; Shooting Star, p. 38.

Cover Photograph: AP/Wide World

CONTENTS

Arnold Schwarzenegger

1
CALIFORNIA'S CRAZY ELECTION

The studio audience settled into their seats for the afternoon taping of Jay Leno's *Tonight Show*. Backstage, superstar Arnold Schwarzenegger waited to be introduced. His guest appearance at the August 7, 2003, program was generating even more interest than usual. This time the action hero was not there to plug his latest movie, *Terminator 3: Rise of the Machines*. He was there to announce a decision he had been wrestling with for weeks.

Schwarzenegger's appearance came at a time when California politics were in turmoil. Almost as soon as Gray Davis was reelected to his second term as governor in 2002, a movement began to remove him from office. Many voters were fed up with California's huge debt, which topped $38 billion. They were angry when their vehicle registration fees tripled and college fees increased. They did not like the cutbacks in health services and were critical of the governor's mismanagement of an energy crisis. Over 1.6 million people signed petitions demanding that the state hold a special election to recall Governor Davis.

For weeks there had been speculation that Schwarzenegger might add his name to the long list of candidates wanting to replace the governor. Still, rumors had spread that he had decided not to run because of his family's opposition. As a member of the powerful Kennedy political family, his wife, Maria Shriver, knew all too well how difficult running for office could be. Political campaigning can turn nasty and can affect a family's privacy and security. Schwarzenegger had said that he would not run without his wife's approval.[1]

Schwarzenegger chose the popular *Tonight Show* to put the issue to rest once and for all. Before the show began, Leno visited with Schwarzenegger backstage and asked one last time about his announcement. "I am bowing out," Schwarzenegger told him.[2]

After Leno delivered his monologue, Schwarzenegger was introduced to the cheering audience. The two men chatted for a few minutes, then Schwarzenegger got serious. "Well, Jay, after thinking for a long time my decision is . . . ," he began. At that moment, the TV picture disappeared and a PLEASE STAND BY sign flashed across the screen. When the picture came back on, Arnold Schwarzenegger was saying, ". . . That's why I decided that way."[3] In reality, no one had missed his announcement. It was merely a joke.

Then Schwarzenegger dropped the bombshell. "I am going to run for governor of the state of California," he declared in his thick Austrian accent.[4] The audience erupted with whoops and cheers.

Schwarzenegger's announcement caught many by surprise, including his chief political adviser, George Gorton. Gorton was watching from the wings, still clutching Schwarzenegger's press release announcing that he had decided not to run. He even wondered at first if the actor was kidding.[5] But Schwarzenegger was quite serious.

"The politicians are fiddling, fumbling and failing," Schwarzenegger

Arnold Schwarzenegger on *The Tonight Show* with host Jay Leno.

told Leno. "The man that is failing the people more than anyone is Gray Davis. He is failing them terribly, and this is why he needs to be recalled and this is why I am going to run for governor."[6]

This was not the first time Schwarzenegger had used the element of surprise to make an impact. It was a technique he often used in bodybuilding competitions to keep his competitors from knowing until the last minute that he was in the contest.

Later, Schwarzenegger admitted that he and his family had been struggling with the decision for several weeks. Finally, his wife told him that she would support him no matter what his decision was.[7] With her acceptance, Schwarzenegger was free to enter the race.

Reaction to Schwarzenegger's announcement was swift. "With Arnold Schwarzenegger in, it's going to become an instant circus," said Barbara O'Connor, a communications professor at California State University at Sacramento. "Anyone who says they know what's going to happen now is crazy."[8]

California senator Diane Feinstein was against recalling Gray Davis and urged her fellow Democrats not to run against him. She thought the government should concentrate on solving its problems instead of wasting time and an estimated $67 million on the recall election. "Sadly, the state is instead going to be engaged in an election that is becoming more and more like a carnival every day," she said.[9]

Even before Schwarzenegger's announcement, the recall election was shaping up to be one of the most bizarre political events in California's history. Anyone who paid the $3,500 filing fee and got sixty-five people to sign a petition could claim a spot on the ballot. This brought out a colorful cast of 135 characters seeking their brief moment in the spotlight. Now Schwarzenegger had joined the political circus, sporting nicknames taken from his movie roles such as "Conan the Candidate," and "The Governator."

"With Arnold Schwarzenegger in, it's going to become an instant circus."

The fact that Schwarzenegger was running for such a high office was incredible. As an immigrant from Austria, he had not been born or raised in the United States. Although he had achieved phenomenal success as a bodybuilder, a movie star, and a businessman, he had never run for an elective office and his political views were unknown to most Californians. He had not taken the usual path of working his way up the political ladder by seeking smaller offices first. Schwarzenegger aimed straight for the top. This was an ambitious goal, as California not only has the largest state economy in the United States, but had an economy which, at that time, was the fifth largest in the entire world.[10]

Only a few of the 135 candidates on the ballot could

be considered serious contenders. Schwarzenegger's biggest challengers were Bill Simon Jr., who had lost to Gray Davis in the November 2002 election; Peter Ueberroth, the former Major League Baseball commissioner and head of the Los Angeles Olympics in 1984; California senator Tom McClintock; and Davis's own lieutenant governor, Cruz Bustamante.

Before his announcement, Schwarzenegger talked to political consultant Bob White. "Before you make the decision, you need to understand that you're going to be under scrutiny of a kind that you've never seen before," White told him.[11]

Schwarzenegger understood the warning. "They're going to throw everything at me," he confided to Leno. "That I have no experience, I'm a womanizer and a terrible guy."[12]

It was certainly not difficult for Schwarzenegger's opponents to find incidents in his past to use against him in the political battle. Stories of his wilder days were found in magazine interviews from years earlier. Voters were reminded that he was a heavy steroid user during his bodybuilding days. The documentary *Pumping Iron* clearly showed him smoking marijuana. "The bottom line is that's what it was in the '70s, that's what I did. I have never touched it since," Schwarzenegger said about his pot smoking. "I lived a certain life, I want everyone to know that's the life I lived. As you grow up and as you become more mature, those things change," he added.[13]

Most damaging was Schwarzenegger's reputation for his offensive behavior with women. Five days before the election, *The Los Angeles Times* reported that six women had accused Schwarzenegger of touching them inappropriately without their permission. The incidents had happened on movie sets and in other settings from the 1970s to 2000.

Schwarzenegger quickly issued an apology. "Yes, it is true that I was on rowdy movie sets and I have done things that were not right that I thought were playful," he admitted. "I now recognize that I have offended people and to those people that I offended, I want to say that I am deeply sorry."[14]

Many voters, especially women, were not satisfied with Schwarzenegger's apology. They did not appreciate his crude sense of humor, especially when it was being used as an excuse for committing sexual harassment.

In spite of Schwarzenegger's shortcomings,

A Cast of Candidates

As soon as California's recall election was announced, candidates scrambled to add their names to the ballot, which grew longer and longer. Some of the names were familiar, such as former child actor Gary Coleman, star of the television situation comedy *Diff'rent Strokes* from 1978 to 1986. The comedian Gallagher was known more for smashing watermelons onstage than for holding political office. The list also included a denture maker, Indian tribal leader, sumo wrestler, prize fighter, and adult movie actress. Most candidates entered the race to promote their own issues. Whether the concern was legalizing ferrets as pets, earthquake safety, or gambling on American Indian reservations, it seemed as if everyone wanted to get an opinion in front of the public.

those who knew him did not doubt that he had the power to win. He displayed the same charm and air of confidence that had been with him since his bodybuilding days. He was also a man who knew how to sell anything, especially himself, even if it required exaggeration or altering facts to fit the situation.

The recall election was held on October 7, 2003. First, voters were asked to choose whether or not Gray Davis should be recalled. Then they voted for one person—the one they would want to replace Davis if the recall passed. Almost as soon as the polls closed, all major networks proclaimed Arnold Schwarzenegger to be the winner. He had captured 49 percent of the vote, more than a million more votes than his closest competitor, Bustamante.

Later that evening, Schwarzenegger stood before a crowd of jubilant supporters. "I came here with absolutely nothing," he told the crowd, "and California has given me absolutely everything. And today, California has given me the greatest gift of all. You have given me your trust by voting for me."[15] "I will not fail you, I will not disappoint you, and I will not let you down."[16]

The voters of California had put their faith in the former bodybuilder and superstar. Only time would tell if the "Governator" would live up to their expectations.

2
SECOND
BEST

By 1947, the mountainous country of Austria was still struggling to recover from World War II. Adolf Hitler, the German Nazi dictator, had been defeated, but the war he caused left most of Europe suffering from widespread poverty and unemployment. Gustav Schwarzenegger joined the Nazi Party and served as a military policeman for the German army. When the war was over, he took a job as the police chief of the tiny farming village of Thal near the city of Graz. He and his wife, Aurelia, settled into the police chief's quarters on the upper floor of a three-hundred-year-old house. Their son Meinhard was born in 1946. Then, on July 30, 1947, Aurelia gave birth to a second son, Arnold Alois Schwarzenegger.

Like the other families of Thal at that time, the

Arnold was born in the village of Thal, near Graz, Austria, in western Europe.

Schwarzeneggers did not have money for luxuries. "It was right after World War II, and the country was absolutely devastated and destroyed. We had no flushing toilet in the house. No refrigerator. What we did have was food rations," Arnold recalled.[1] "Nobody had a phone except the village restaurant, the priest and the police station, where my father worked. There was one TV set, in the village restaurant."[2]

Peace may have come to Austria, but it was not always present in the Schwarzenegger household. Gustav was a harsh disciplinarian who raised his sons in a strict, military fashion. He demanded good grades in school and exceptional athletic ability. The boys were required to do squats and sit-ups for fifteen minutes every morning to earn their breakfast. They polished their father's shoes and the brass belt of his uniform until they glistened. If their job did not meet with Gustav's approval, the boys would have to do it over.

Three-year-old Arnold, with his mother and his brother, Meinhard.

Arnold, age eleven, worked hard at school. His father demanded excellence.

The family often went on outings to museums, concerts, and other events, but there was a downside. After each outing, Gustav required Arnold and Meinhard to write ten-page reports describing in detail what they had seen. He graded their essays, covering their papers with ugly red marks to point out their shortcomings in spelling and grammar. Gustav's domineering personality became even worse when he had too much to drink, which happened often.

Life was especially hard for Arnold. From the beginning, he knew that his brother was their father's favorite. Gustav constantly pitted the boys against each other in everything from academics to athletics. After each competition, Gustav would ask the loser, "Tell me which one of you was the best?"[3]

It was usually Arnold who had to bitterly admit out loud that his brother was better than he was. The humiliation took its toll. "I always felt I wasn't good enough, smart enough, strong enough, that I hadn't accomplished enough," Arnold said later.[4]

The one place Arnold could go to forget his troubles at home was the movie theater in Graz. He especially liked the films his father did not want him to see. Sometimes he would sneak into the theater by walking in backward as everyone else was leaving.[5] He sat in the dark and watched Reg Park and Steve Reeves in the heroic roles of Hercules and Tarzan. Both men were bodybuilders whose well-developed muscles made them look powerful. Most of Arnold's friends liked Reeves the best, but Arnold favored Park's strong, rugged look.[6]

Athletics had always been important to Gustav. At one time he had been Austria's curling champion. Curling is a game where large stones are slid across an ice rink toward a goal. Gustav encouraged his sons to become involved in sports. Arnold began playing soccer at age ten, but after a few years he felt that something was missing. Although the team received recognition when it did well, Arnold longed for more personal glory. He tried individual sports, such as running, swimming, and boxing, but none of them gave him the pleasure he was looking for.

When Arnold was fifteen, his soccer coach suggested that the boys train in a gym once a week to strengthen their legs. Arnold became fascinated by the weightlifters with their massive, well-defined muscles. They had a powerful, Herculean look. Something clicked inside Arnold. For the first time, he knew exactly what he wanted to do with his life.

"I always felt I wasn't good enough, smart enough, strong enough."

During the summer, some of the bodybuilders helped Arnold get his body ready for workouts in the gym. They spent their time at the lake doing sit-ups, push-ups, chin-ups, and other exercises without weights.

Finally, Arnold was ready to begin formal training. On his first day, he rode his bicycle eight miles to Graz. He lifted barbells and dumbbells and worked out on weight machines. The older lifters told him to slow down so that he would not get sore, but Arnold could not stop. It was not until he headed for home that he understood their warnings. "I started riding home and fell off my bike. I was so weak I couldn't make my hands hold on. I had no feeling in my legs: they were noodles. I was numb, my whole body buzzing," Arnold said later.[7] He ended up pushing his bike all the way home. The next morning his muscles were so stiff, he could not even raise his arms to comb his hair. At breakfast he spilled coffee all over the table because he could not hold his cup.

Arnold did not care about stiff muscles. He had found his passion, and nothing was going to stand in his way. He began training three days a week at the Graz Athletic Union, a dingy gym tucked into the corner of the soccer stadium. The gym had bare cement floors, no heat, and only a minimal number of weights and equipment. In the winter, newspapers were stuffed into a hole in the wall to keep out the frigid air, but when the wind blew hard, the paper blew out. It once got so cold that the skin on Arnold's hands froze onto the bars.

When Arnold started training, he was six feet tall and weighed 150 pounds. "He had very bad posture, a slightly shrunken chest, fallen shoulders, and very skinny legs," said trainer Helmut Cerncic.[8] But his confidence was as big as Austria. He had not been training very long when he announced to another bodybuilder "Well, I give myself about five years and I will be Mr. Universe." Everyone thought he was crazy.[9]

Arnold did not care what the others thought. He knew he was going to succeed. He studied muscle magazines, such as *Muscle Builder* and *Mr. America*, and hung pictures of his heroes on his bedroom wall. Many of the pictures were of his idol, Reg Park. Arnold admired the way Park had turned his bodybuilding success into movie roles, then used his earnings to build a gym empire.

"Bingo! I had my role model! If he could do it, I could do it!" said Arnold. "I'd win Mr. Universe. I'd become a movie star. I'd get rich. One, two, three—bing, bang, boom! I found my passion. I got my goal."[10]

Even at that young age, Arnold had an incredible ability for setting goals and working to reach them. "I set a goal, visualize it very clearly, and create the drive, the hunger, for turning it into reality. There's a kind of joy in that kind of ambition, in having a vision in front of you," Arnold explained later.[11]

With his goal firmly planted in his mind, Arnold used his fierce determination to achieve it. He was not bothered by the pain that came with his intense training. To him, it was a sign that his muscles were growing. He did not even care if he fainted.

"I have no fear of fainting," he said. "I do squats until I fall over and pass out. So what? It's not going to kill me. I wake up five minutes later and I'm okay. A lot of other athletes are afraid of this. So they don't pass out."[12]

When Arnold increased his training to six days a week, his father became concerned about his son's obsession with weightlifting. At that time bodybuilding was an unpopular sport. Bodybuilders were considered freaks. But Arnold did not care. He did not want to be normal. "Normal people can be happy with a regular life. I was different. I felt there was more to life than just

> "I felt there was **more** to life than just plodding through an **average** existence."

plodding through an average existence. I'd always been impressed by stories of greatness and power. I wanted to do something special, to be recognized as the best," Arnold said.[13]

Gustav tried to slow Arnold down by allowing him to go to the gym only three times a week. Arnold got around his father's rules by building his own gym in the unheated basement of their house. Some nights, when Gustav was asleep, Arnold hitchhiked down the mountain to the gym in Graz, where he trained for several hours. When there were no cars on the road afterward to give him a ride home, he hiked back to Thal, arriving early in the morning.

"People at the gym were inspired by his dedication. He was also admired for his enthusiasm and devilish sense of humor. Arnold liked to have fun. His laugh was

Anabolic Steroids

It was Arnold's hard work that made his muscles grow, but he got some help from anabolic steroids. These drugs, which can increase strength and body weight, were legal when Arnold began taking them. He was introduced to steroids by his trainer, a former Mr. Austria, Kurt Marnul. "There were no weightlifters in the world who did not take them. You could get prescriptions for them from the doctor. Arnold never took them, though, without my supervision," Marnul said.[14]

Today we know about the dangerous side effects of anabolic steroids. They can cause liver damage, tumors, infertility, acne, and uncontrolled aggression called "roid rage." Some athletes have died from their use. Steroids can be especially harmful to teenagers, whose bodies are still maturing. The powerful hormones can slow their growth so that they never reach their full height.

Since virtually all competitive bodybuilders in those days used anabolic steroids, it is unlikely that Arnold could have become a champion without them. However, his success came primarily from training longer and harder than everyone else to perfect his muscles and his poses.

his trademark," remembered Karl Kainrath, a fellow bodybuilder.[15]

In spite of Arnold's lack of interest in academics, he graduated from high school when he reached eighteen. He joined the Austrian army for his year of mandatory service. He wanted to drive a tank, but the army required tank drivers to be at least twenty-one years of age. Also, Arnold was too tall to fit comfortably in a tank. Even so, Gustav used his influence to get his son assigned to the tank division in Graz.

Arnold enjoyed the army. He was already used to rigid structure and discipline. He liked the uniforms and medals and some of the other trappings of the military. But one rule stood in the way of his goal.

Soon after Arnold joined the army, he received an invitation to compete in the Junior Mr. Europe contest. Young bodybuilders considered this the biggest event of the year. Since Arnold was in basic training, he was not allowed to leave the base. To make matters worse, the contest was being held in Stuttgart, Germany, a day away by train. After giving it much thought, Arnold decided that not even the Austrian Army could keep him from going to this competition. He decided to go AWOL (absent without leave).

The day before the competition, Arnold sneaked out of the base and caught the overnight train to Stuttgart. He arrived tired from the long trip and nervous about being in his first big competition.[16] He had come with only the clothes on his back and had to borrow posing trunks and body oil from another contestant.

Arnold had prepared the best he could for his competition. He had practiced the poses Reg Park used in photographs in muscle magazines. He breezed through the first round and made it to the finals. Arnold flexed his muscles again in a series of poses, then waited for the results. Finally, the judges handed him the trophy as winner of the title Junior Mr. Europe for 1965. He was the first person to ever receive an ideal score, which was three hundred points at that time.

The crowd cheered, and Arnold was showered with attention. "I knew for certain that I was on the way to becoming the world's greatest bodybuilder. I felt I was already one of the best in the world. Obviously, I wasn't even in the top 5,000; but in my mind I was the best," Arnold said.[17]

When Arnold arrived back at the base, he was arrested and put in the army's jail. He did not care. Winning his first big competition was worth any punishment the army could give him. By the time Arnold was released a week later, he had become a hero on the base. He had even won the admiration of his superior officers who saw his success as a way to bring glory to Austria. They rearranged his

> "I **knew** for certain that I was on the **way** to becoming the world's **greatest** bodybuilder.

Arnold sneaked away from his army base to compete in the 1965 Junior Mr. Europe competition. He won with a perfect score.

schedule to allow him to continue his training. He worked with tanks in the morning and trained in the afternoon. The army also gave him all the food he wanted to eat. Pound by pound, muscle by muscle, Arnold built up the impressive physique that earned him the nickname the Austrian Oak. By the time he finished his year of military service, he had packed another twenty-five pounds of muscle on to his frame.

Arnold left the army when his year was up. His parents urged him to quit his useless hobby of bodybuilding and get a respectable job. He could become a policeman like his father, or attend trade school, or even stay in the army. But there was no way this ambitious young man would be happy with a normal life. Visions of greatness burned in his mind. The only way he could reach his goals was to leave Austria behind.

3
MOVING ON

hen Schwarzenegger stepped off the train in Munich, Germany, he entered a new and exciting world. People hurried down the crowded sidewalks in the shadows of tall buildings. Noisy traffic rumbled through the streets. The large bustling city was a dramatic change from Graz, but Schwarzenegger knew this was the place for him.[1]

Schwarzenegger moved into a small apartment and began working as a trainer at a gym. His job included more sweeping and mopping than actual training. Still, it allowed him to pay his expenses while pursuing his goals. Juggling his intense workouts with his job led him to a more efficient training method. By splitting his training into two shorter sessions—two hours in the morning and two in the evenings—he was able to do more and get faster results.

For Schwarzenegger, the bustling city of Munich was a big change from his rural childhood home.

In September 1966, Schwarzenegger won the Mr. Europe title. Contest officials offered to pay his way to the Mr. Universe contest in London. Unfortunately, they took back their offer the next week when he won the title of Best Built Man in Europe, sponsored by a rival federation. His friends came to his rescue and helped him raise enough money to pay for his plane ticket.

Schwarzenegger's flight to London for the Mr. Universe contest was his first time in an airplane. It was not a comfortable experience. "When I heard the landing gear come up with a shudder into the body of the plane, it was like a cold fist closing on my heart. I was certain we were gone," he said later.[2]

Schwarzenegger arrived in London as a green nineteen-year-old kid to compete against older and more experienced bodybuilders. Any thoughts he had of winning the competition disappeared when he saw Chet Yorton from the United States. Yorton's muscles were not just large, they were sharply defined and topped with bulging veins showing that there was no fat between the muscle and the skin. Most of all, Yorton radiated a winning attitude. Yorton was named Mr. Universe, while Schwarzenegger finished second, a much higher placement than his friends had expected.

Back in Munich, the man Schwarzenegger worked for decided to sell his gym. Schwarzenegger worked extra jobs and borrowed from friends to raise the money he needed to buy the gym himself. Then, by publicizing his second-place finish in the Mr. Universe contest, he increased membership from seventy members to two hundred in a short time.

Schwarzenegger realized that in order to reach his goal of becoming Mr. Universe he would have to build up his calves and thighs. For motivation, he cut his trousers off at the knees so the other weight lifters would make fun of his legs. He stepped up his training, confident that next time the Mr. Universe title would be his.

"What I had more than anyone else was drive," Schwarzenegger said. "I was hungrier than anybody. I wanted it so badly it hurt. I knew there could be no one else in the world who wanted this title as much as I did."[3]

That fall, Wag Bennett, a judge for Mr. Universe, invited Schwarzenegger to his home in London. Bennett and his wife taught Schwarzenegger the finer points of posing so he could do exhibitions. They encouraged him to mix showmanship with bodybuilding. When they suggested that he add music to his routine, he began posing to the stirring theme from the movie *Exodus*. After two days of practice, Schwarzenegger tried out his new routine in front of a London audience. When he finished, the audience kept cheering. People asked him for his autograph and treated him like a star.

While Schwarzenegger was in London, Bennett

> **"What I had more than anyone else was drive."**

asked him to define his life's ambition. Schwarzenegger's answer surprised him. Unlike most bodybuilders, whose goals rarely extended past the next title they hoped to win, Schwarzenegger's goals were a laundry list of accomplishments ready to be checked off one by one. He would go to America and become the greatest bodybuilder in history. He would invest the money he earned in real estate. He would get into movies as an actor, producer, and director and would attend college to earn a business degree. He would become a millionaire by the time he was thirty, and would marry a glamorous and intelligent wife.[4]

In January 1967, Bennett introduced Arnold Schwarzenegger to Reg Park at a gym in London. Schwarzenegger was nervous about meeting his boyhood movie idol and role model. At first, he felt self-conscious and unsure

Picking a Winner

In competitions, bodybuilders are judged by how their bodies look and how they are presented. First, judges evaluate the *symmetry*, or overall shape and proportion, of the contestant's body. Someone with good symmetry has wide shoulders, well-developed back muscles, tapering to smaller waist and hips.

Judges also look at the contestant's *definition*, also known as *muscularity* or *cuts*. If a bodybuilder has almost no body fat, each muscle group can be seen so clearly that even the small grooves in the muscles, called *striations*, are visible. Each muscle can be seen separately, making the contestant with good definition look like a walking anatomy chart.

As long as the muscles have good definition and the body has good symmetry, then muscle *mass*, or size, is a plus. Presentation is also important. Contestants develop poses designed to show off their muscles in the best way. Even having a good tan helps. Pale skin can looked washed out under stage lights, making muscle definition harder to see.

Schwarzenegger competed in bodybuilding competitions all over Europe, winning most of them.

of what to say, especially since he did not speak much English. But once his original anxiety was gone, the two men became friends. Schwarzenegger learned a lot from Park as they traveled to Ireland and several cities in England, giving exhibitions. Park even said he would like the young bodybuilder to visit him in South Africa, but only after Schwarzenegger won the Mr. Universe title.

Schwarzenegger went back to Munich and trained furiously until it was time to go to London for the 1967 Mr. Universe competition. He was only twenty years old, but he had a body worthy of competing against even the most seasoned competitors. Packed on to his six-foot-two-inch frame were 235 pounds of sculpted muscle. His flexed biceps measured twenty-two inches and his chest expanded to fifty-seven inches, then narrowed to a thirty-four-inch waist. Schwarzenegger beat out ninety other bodybuilders from all over the world to become the youngest Mr. Universe in history.

He had reached his goal, but for Schwarzenegger, that was only the beginning. There were other competitions and other champions he would have to conquer before he was finished. He had just won the amateur Mr. Universe sponsored by the National Amateur Bodybuilders Association (NABBA), but there was also a professional Mr. Universe and another one sponsored by the IFBB (International Federation of Body Builders). The Mr. World and Mr. Olympia titles also needed to be captured. Schwarzenegger would not quit until he won them all and became recognized as the best bodybuilder in the world.

Reg Park was true to his word and invited the newest Mr. Universe to visit his estate in Johannesburg, South Africa. Park's luxurious home had a swimming pool in front and was furnished with expensive antiques. The house was surrounded by acres of beautiful trees and flowers. Spending time with Park gave Schwarzenegger a firsthand look at what his own life could be.

In 1968 Schwarzenegger won the Mr. Universe professional title in London. Word of the young athlete's success reached Joe Weider in the United States. Weider, along with his brother Ben, had dedicated their lives to promoting bodybuilding as a respected sport. Weider published bodybuilding magazines and sold nutritional supplements and bodybuilding equipment. "I kept hearing about this massive young athlete, so I asked my European associates to find out more about him," Weider said. "I already knew that someone like Schwarzenegger would be very beneficial for our sport."[5]

Weider invited Schwarzenegger to America to compete in the IFBB Mr. Universe contest in Miami, Florida. Here was Schwarzenegger's chance to check another goal off his list—to go to America.

Schwarzenegger arrived in Miami with only a gym bag and a small amount of money in his pocket. He did not speak much English, could not read the newspapers or even listen to the news. Still, he came full of confidence, ready to win Mr. Universe—until he saw the American bodybuilders. Their sharply-defined muscles and their smooth poses proved to be tough competition.

Schwarzenegger came in second place, losing to American Frank Zane. He admitted that Zane deserved to win. "He had all the qualities it took to be Mr. Universe—the muscularity, the separation, the definition, the skin color, the glow of confidence. He was finished like a piece of sculpture ready to be put on display."[6]

Schwarzenegger was miserable that night. He was far from home and in a strange country with people speaking a strange language and he had just lost an important competition. He cried himself to sleep. For that moment, at least, the American dream seemed more like a nightmare. But soon Schwarzenegger had his determination back and was ready to work even harder to become the world's best bodybuilder.

Weider agreed to sponsor Schwarzenegger for one year. He paid him $100 a week and gave him an apartment in California, a car, and the chance to train at Gold's gym with some of the best bodybuilders in the world. In return, Schwarzenegger agreed to write articles for Weider's magazines and promote his supplements and equipment. "I knew at that time that he would be a great champion," Weider said later. "He was charming, he made you laugh, and he trained hard, and he was totally dedicated."[7]

In the fall of 1969, Schwarzenegger went to New York City for the IFBB Mr. Universe contest. He was disappointed to find that Cuban bodybuilder Sergio Oliva was not competing. Oliva had won the Mr. Olympia title two years in a row and was considered one of the best bodybuilders in the business. Instead of competing in the Mr. Universe contest, Oliva was in Miami getting ready to defend his title that night.

Schwarzenegger would never be considered the best until he beat Oliva, and he was too impatient to wait any longer. He called Miami and got permission to register late for the competition.

Schwarzenegger won the Mr. Universe title in New York in the afternoon, with all the judges giving him first place. He collected his trophy, then immediately flew to

Miami to compete for Mr. Olympia that night. The Mr. Olympia competition was considered the Super Bowl of bodybuilding. It was open only to winners of other contests.

When Schwarzenegger arrived at the competition, he saw Oliva relaxing in the dressing room, wearing overalls. At first, Oliva did not look too threatening, but when he took off his overalls and started pumping up, Schwarzenegger realized what he was up against. Oliva casually flexed his massive muscles in front of Schwarzenegger. "His back muscles were so huge that he seemed to be as wide as the hall itself!" Schwarzenegger recalled.[8]

"Right there and then I knew it was all over for me. I was completely psyched out. He took away my determination to beat him. When I went out to pose it was just a matter of going through the motions. I'd lost the contest before I stepped onstage."[9] Schwarzenegger's second place finish made him even more determined to beat Oliva the next time.

The following weekend, Schwarzenegger flew to London for the NABBA Mr. Universe competition. He easily picked up his fourth Mr. Universe title, his second in just a matter of weeks. It was still not enough for Schwarzenegger. His desire to defeat Oliva burned inside him and fueled his determination to train harder.

Weider agreed to let Schwarzenegger stay in California for another year and even brought over his best friend and training partner, Franco Columbu. Schwarzenegger resumed his intense training schedule, knowing that the next time he would crush Oliva.

Schwarzenegger knew that bodybuilding alone would not bring him the wealth he wanted. He took business courses by correspondence from the University of Wisconsin-Superior. He also learned a great deal by working with Weider in his profitable publishing empire. Schwarzenegger set up his own mail order business to sell body-building aids and instructional booklets.

"Right there and then I knew it was all over for me."

Schwarzenegger had always looked up to Reg Park, so it was a bittersweet moment in 1970 when he defeated his boyhood idol in London by capturing his fifth Mr. Universe title. Schwarzenegger picked up his trophy, then jetted back to the United States for the Mr. World competition being held in Columbus, Ohio, the next day.

Schwarzenegger arrived in Columbus worn out from twelve hours of traveling and a five-hour time difference. He was not expecting much competition and thought he would win easily. But there was a surprise waiting for him in Columbus—Sergio Oliva. Schwarzenegger had not expected to face Oliva until the Mr. Olympia contest two weeks later. In spite of fatigue and jet lag, his year of intense training paid off. He defeated Oliva for the first time and earned the title of Mr. World.

Moving to the United States was one of Schwarzenegger's dreams and goals.

During the competition for the Mr. World title, Schwarzenegger became impressed with the way sports promoter Jim Lorimer had organized the event. He told Lorimer that he wanted to be his partner. "When I am done competing in the sport of bodybuilding I want to go into the promotion of the sport, raise the image of the sport and I am going to raise the cash-prizes up to 100,000 dollars and make it a very professional sport," Schwarzenegger told him.[10]

Schwarzenegger had just won $500 as winner of Mr. World. Raising the prize money to $100,000 seemed like an impossible dream, but Lorimer agreed. He was not sure anything would come of it. He did not know that Schwarzenegger was used to making his plans five years in advance.

Competition is tough among the top bodybuilders. It is common for competitors to try to get ahead by using mind games and tricks. Psyching out opponents, which Schwarzenegger refers to as "gamesmanship," is a way of shaking their confidence or concentration so they will not perform as well. Some see this as poor sportsmanship or cheating. Schwarzenegger sees it as taking advantage of an opponent's psychological weakness to gain an edge in the competition.[11] Although Schwarzenegger was on the receiving end of some of this psychological warfare, he was especially good at dishing it out.

Two weeks after Mr. World, Schwarzenegger again met Oliva in the Mr. Olympia contest in New York. The finals featured Schwarzenegger and Oliva posing side by side. After a while, Schwarzenegger told Oliva that he was finished, and the two men began to leave the stage. After Oliva left, Schwarzenegger turned to the audience for one last pose. He believes that the judges assumed Oliva had given up and awarded the victory to Schwarzenegger.

Schwarzenegger had reached his goal of beating Oliva, but he still had other things he planned to accomplish in his life. One ambition was to be in movies. Surprisingly, he received help from an unlikely source— his fictional childhood hero, Hercules.

Schwarzenegger broke into film by starring in *Hercules in New York*.

4
HERCULES OPENS
A DOOR

In 1970, Joe Weider got a call from a movie company.
They needed a bodybuilder to play the mythical
Greek hero Hercules in a low-budget film. Weider
knew that Schwarzenegger had an interest in being in the
movies, and he certainly had the physical build for the part.
"They asked me if he could act," Weider recalled. "I said,
'Of course he can. In England he was a Shakespearean
actor.' And they fell for it."[1]

Weider knew that Schwarzenegger had never been an
actor, but his trick worked. Schwarzenegger was hired for
the part, and the seeds of his movie career were planted.

Hercules in New York, first titled *Hercules Goes Bananas*,
was a forgettable film made for Italian television.
Schwarzenegger played the part of Hercules, a god from
Mount Olympus, on a visit to New York City. Hercules

bumbles his way through the big city dressed mostly in a toga, taking on mobsters and pro-wrestling promoters. His most memorable scene had him driving a chariot around Central Park.

At that time, few people had heard of Arnold Schwarzenegger, and *Hercules* did nothing to change that. The producers thought his name was too much of a mouthful, so it was changed to Arnold Strong. Even his voice did not make it in to the film. His lines were dubbed by someone speaking Italian. Although it was not great, at least Schwarzenegger had his first movie under his belt.

Tragedy hit Schwarzenegger's family on May 20, 1971. His brother Meinhard was driving drunk when he crashed into another car and was killed instantly. Schwarzenegger had grown up in Meinhard's shadow, always knowing that his brother was the favored child. But in the end, it was Schwarzenegger who became successful while his brother struggled. Meinhard had acquired his father's dependence on alcohol and was often drunk. He could not hold down a job, sank into depression, and had minor scrapes with the law.

Schwarzenegger did not go home for the funeral, but he offered to help support Meinhard's young son, Patrick. When Patrick was older, Schwarzenegger paid for his schooling and eventually brought him to the United States to finish his education.

Schwarzenegger continued to push ahead on all

aspects of his life's plan, including his goal to be rich. He did exhibitions and invested his earnings in real estate. Columbu remembers doing several shows in South Africa with him in 1971. Schwarzenegger refused to spend any of the money he earned from the exhibitions.

When he got home, he used every penny to buy a six-unit apartment building. Later, he sold it for a profit and bought a bigger one. He was on his way to becoming a real estate mogul while still working to become the best bodybuilder in the world.

> **Schwarzenegger pushed ahead on all aspects of his life's plan, including his goal to be rich.**

At the Mr. Olympia contest in 1972, Schwarzenegger was once again up against Sergio Oliva. When Schwarzenegger arrived, no one had decided which room to use for the preliminaries. Schwarzenegger looked at all the rooms and chose the one with dark paint in the background. "It hadn't occurred to Sergio that my white body would stand out against the dark wall behind us, while his would blend right in. To this day, I believe that was how I got the edge," Schwarzenegger said.[2]

Schwarzenegger traveled to Essen, Germany, for the Mr. Olympia 1972 competition. This contest was special because Schwarzenegger's father came to see him compete. Schwarzenegger had the joy of showing his father that he was a winner, but that joy was short lived. Gustav

Pumping Up Prisoners

As America's leading bodybuilder, Schwarzenegger received letters from fans asking for training tips. Some of the letters came from prison inmates. Schwarzenegger saw a need for them to have something positive to focus on while they were locked up. He felt that weightlifting was something that could build up their self-image while they were in prison and could be continued when they got out. Schwarzenegger designed bodybuilding programs for the inmates and volunteered his time as a trainer.

Some people thought it was risky to make prisoners stronger and more imposing than they already were. Schwarzenegger disagreed. "Weight training has the opposite effect. Steam is let off, hostile feelings and stress are replaced by a more positive outlook on life," he said.[4]

Schwarzenegger died of a stroke two months later, at the age of sixty-five. Once again, Arnold chose not go home for the funeral, for reasons that are unclear.

While competing at the Mr. America contest in New York City in 1972, Schwarzenegger met someone who would make a big impact on his life. George Butler was a photographer working with author Charles Gaines on a book titled *Pumping Iron.* The book was an inside look at the world of bodybuilding. Butler and Gaines had done most of the background research, but they needed a central character in order to present their information on a more personal level. When they met Arnold Schwarzenegger, they knew they had found their subject. "Arnold is like the Matterhorn," Gaines commented. "We didn't discover him, we just noticed him first."[3]

When *Pumping Iron* came out, *The New York Times* declined to review it. They thought a book of pictures of half-dressed musclemen would not interest many people. Two months later, *Pumping Iron* was on the best-seller list. The book humanized the world of bodybuilding and gave credibility to the misunderstood sport. It also introduced Arnold Schwarzenegger to millions of people who had never heard of him before.

In 1973, Schwarzenegger appeared in his second movie. He had a small part playing a goon who terrorized a private eye, Philip Marlowe, in *The Long Goodbye*. Schwarzenegger did not have to speak. He just stood around looking large and threatening.

In 1975, comedienne Lucille Ball saw Schwarzenegger on a talk show. She liked his charm and humor and invited him to be on her television special, called *Happy Anniversary and Good-bye*. She arranged for Schwarzenegger to take acting lessons for a week and even directed him herself. Schwarzenegger played an Italian masseur who was hired to help Lucy's girlfriend get into shape.

The success of the book *Pumping Iron* led George Butler to film a feature-length docudrama by the same name. The movie followed Schwarzenegger and several other bodybuilders as they prepared for the 1975 Mr. Olympia competition in Pretoria, South Africa. Much of the movie was true, while other aspects were exaggerated for dramatic effect. The contest was real, with Schwarzenegger winning his sixth Mr. Olympia title. He defeated Lou Ferrigno, who later gained fame as

Dancer Marianne Claire taught Schwarzenegger some ballet moves during the filming of the documentary *Pumping Iron*.

the Hulk in the *Incredible Hulk* TV series. With the cameras rolling, Schwarzenegger accepted his trophy from Reg Park, then made a startling announcement.

"I would like to announce officially that I am retiring from bodybuilding competition. Bodybuilding has been a beautiful experience for me and I will continue it for the rest of my life. I only stopped competing but I am not stopping bodybuilding. It is the greatest sport."[5]

By then, Schwarzenegger was twenty-eight and was the undisputed bodybuilding champion of the world. He had won an extraordinary thirteen world titles and defeated all the top competitors in the world. The *Guinness Book of World Records* had named him the most perfectly developed man in the history of the world. There was nothing else for him to prove in the sport of bodybuilding. Along the way he had built up an international fan base and had shown the world his charisma. Pursuing his dream of becoming a movie star was the next logical step.

"I realized that I was really an entertainer, that I needed to develop another area where I could perform," Schwarzenegger says. "So I just went after it—acting."[6]

With that, Schwarzenegger gathered up his boundless self-confidence and determination and headed for his next goal—movie star.

5 NEW CHALLENGES

Schwarzenegger was finally free from the demands of competing for bodybuilding titles, but he was far from turning his back on the sport. Five years earlier, he and Jim Lorimer had agreed to become partners in promoting bodybuilding, and that is exactly what Schwarzenegger intended to do. On his way home from the Mr. Olympia competition in Africa, he stopped in Columbus, Ohio, where he and Lorimer finalized their partnership. The next year the two men began running several of the major competitions, including Mr. Olympia, Mr. Universe, and Mr. World.

Schwarzenegger began focusing on his dream of becoming a screen star. It was not going to be easy. Two agents refused to take him on as a client. Schwarzenegger recalled that they said to him, "Arnold, you have a weird body and you have a weird accent. Everything about you is so strange, you're never going to make it in this industry."[1] Others suggested that he change his name because Schwarzenegger was too long and hard to pronounce. Arnold Schwarzenegger reacted in his usual way. He became more determined than ever to succeed to prove them wrong.

> **Schwarzenegger began focusing on his dream of becoming a screen star. It was not going to be easy.**

In 1976, a movie came along that was a perfect fit for Schwarzenegger. Director Bob Rafelson needed someone to play the part of an Austrian bodybuilder in the movie *Stay Hungry*. At first, Rafelson was against using an unknown actor for one of the leading roles. But when he met Schwarzenegger, he changed his mind. Before filming started, Rafelson had Schwarzenegger take twelve weeks of lessons with acting coach Eric Morris.

Schwarzenegger threw himself into acting lessons with his usual drive and dedication. He even learned how to play awkward love scenes with petite Sally Field. When he found out that his character played the violin, he took two months of violin lessons to make his movements convincing on film. Schwarzenegger's appearance in *Stay Hungry* helped establish him as a legitimate actor and netted him a Golden Globe Award for the most promising newcomer of the year.

The "most promising newcomer" holds up his Golden Globe award.

When the movie *Pumping Iron* opened on January 18, 1977, it became a surprise hit. Filmgoers got a glimpse into the lives of world-class champions with their demanding training schedules, special diets, and drive for perfection. But it was seeing that these athletes had the same fears, ambitions, and desires as other men that humanized the sport. *Pumping Iron* brought bodybuilding out of the shadows and made Schwarzenegger a role model for those who wanted to improve themselves.

Schwarzenegger had been writing articles for Joe Weider's magazines for many years. Now the time seemed right for him to write a book of his own. He teamed up with Douglas Kent Hall to write *Arnold: Education of a Bodybuilder*. The book was part autobiography and part training manual.

Schwarzenegger was not shy about marketing his first book. When his publisher, Simon and

The Art of Muscles

When the filming of *Pumping Iron* was done, George Butler was left with a hundred hours of film that had to be cut down to ninety minutes, and a $35,000 credit card bill with no financial backers to help him out. In a daring move, he got the prestigious Whitney Museum of American Art in New York City to hold a living exhibit called "Articulate Muscle: the Body as Art." The museum expected about three hundred people to show up for the unusual exhibit. Surprisingly, nearly three thousand spectators crowded into the museum to admire the physiques of Arnold Schwarzenegger, Frank Zane, and Ed Corney. It was the largest crowd the museum had drawn for a single event.[2] As a result of the successful show, Butler got the financial backing he needed, *Pumping Iron* was released, and bodybuilding gained a lot of new fans.

Schuster, offered to send him on a promotional tour to seven cities, Schwarzenegger talked them into expanding the tour to thirty cities. "I wanted to go out and do something unique and different and not just do the traditional way of marketing. They got out my book into sporting-goods stores, which never happened before, and I went to thirty cities and we made our book a bestseller."[3]

Arnold Schwarzenegger did not play tennis, but that did not keep him from accepting an invitation to play in the Robert F. Kennedy Pro-Celebrity Tennis Tournament in Forest Hills, New York, in

Former football star Rosie Greer teamed up with Schwarzenegger at the Robert F. Kennedy Pro-Celebrity Tennis Tournament.

1977. He and retired football player Rosie Greer took on a couple of youngsters. The two men hammed it up for the audience and eventually beat their two young opponents.

Many members of the Kennedy family attended the tournament, including Maria Shriver, niece of the late president John F. Kennedy. Shriver had just graduated from Georgetown University with a degree in American Studies. She had no desire to follow her famous relatives into politics and chose to pursue a career in television journalism instead.

There was an instant attraction between Shriver and Schwarzenegger. "She was filled with all kinds of dreams and ambitions. I was taken with her sense of humor and absolute joy," Schwarzenegger said. "I knew instantly that Maria was *the* woman for my life, she was so *full* of life. I loved her drive to succeed, among her other great qualities."[4]

Shriver liked the fact that Schwarzenegger was a self-made man. "I am absolutely fascinated by people who overcome whatever limitations they might have had to achieve their dreams," she said.[5]

> "I knew **instantly** that Maria was *the* woman for my life."

While Shriver was captivated with Schwarzenegger, her family and friends were not thrilled with the match. "Everyone had a problem with Arnold," Shriver said. "I don't know one person who thought he was a good idea. They had never met anyone like him. So I was on a pretty lonely island there."[6]

Schwarzenegger had never met a family quite like Shriver's. It seemed as if their entire lives were centered on helping others. Shriver's father, Sargent Shriver, began the Peace Corps in 1961 to help people in underdeveloped countries. Shriver's mother, Eunice Shriver, started Special Olympics in 1968 to give mentally disabled children a chance to succeed at sports.

Schwarzenegger had spent years focusing on himself to become a champion bodybuilder and film star. Meeting Shriver's family opened his eyes. When Eunice Shriver introduced him to Special Olympics, he volunteered to be the honorary weightlifting coach. He created a weightlifting program and used his celebrity status to raise money for equipment. Eventually, he became the International Weight Training Coach and served as a Global Ambassador for the organization.

Schwarzenegger's work with the Special Olympics brought him a benefit that he did not expect. "You go into training thinking that you are going to impress them, but the fact is when you walk out of there, you feel inspired," he said.[7]

Schwarzenegger and Shriver had one very big difference.

> **Schwarzenegger's work with the Special Olympics brought him a benefit that he did not expect.**

Politically, Schwarzenegger was a conservative Republican while Shriver came from a long line of liberal Democrats. Shriver once told her uncle the Democratic Senator Ted Kennedy, "Don't look at him as a Republican. Look at him as the man I love. And if that doesn't work, look at him as someone who can squash you."[8]

> **"You go into training thinking that you are going to impress them, but the fact is when you walk out of there, you feel inspired."**

Schwarzenegger and Shriver began a long-distance courtship. Shriver took a job as a trainee in broadcast journalism at a television station in Philadelphia. Schwarzenegger's film career kept him in California and various film locations. They tried to get together on weekends as much as possible. One weekend in 1979, Shriver was on hand to witness Schwarzenegger's graduation from the University of Wisconsin with a degree in business and international economics.

Schwarzenegger continued making movies, but they were a long way from being blockbusters. In 1979 his painfully unfunny movie *The Villain* was released. Some reviewers compared it to a Roadrunner cartoon with live actors and implied that Schwarzenegger's nickname the "Austrian Oak" also described his acting ability.[9] Others called it the worst film of the seventies.

After the stinging failure of *The Villain,*

More than fifteen years after Schwarzenegger graduated from the University of Wisconsin, he returned to receive an honorary doctorate degree.

Schwarzenegger accepted a part he was more at home with. In the docudrama *The Jayne Mansfield Story*, Schwarzenegger played Mickey Hargitay, the Hungarian bodybuilder married to actress Jayne Mansfield. Like Schwarzenegger, Hargitay was a former Mr. Universe. He had won the title in 1956 before bodybuilding was considered respectable. When he married the glamorous Mansfield, his life became overshadowed by her fame. In public he was considered little more than her bodyguard. The movie aired on network television in 1980.

Schwarzenegger had no intentions of giving up his dream of stardom. He took more acting lessons from Eric Morris, but did not enjoy the exercises of trying to dig up unpleasant feelings and memories. He finally stopped taking the classes. "I don't care if I ever become an actor, I'm going to become a star, and everyone is going to know the name Schwarzenegger," he told Betty Weider. "I know how to become a star. Maybe I don't have the talent to become an actor, but I'll become a star."[10]

It had been ten years since Schwarzenegger made his first screen appearance in *Hercules in New York*. He had enjoyed some successes with *Stay Hungry* and *Pumping Iron*, and some disasters, such as *The Villain*. Although he was more well known, movie star-dom had escaped him. Soon, a mythical hero from the Dark Ages would give him the boost he needed.

> **"Maybe I don't have the talent to become an actor, but I'll become a star."**

When Schwarzenegger came out of retirement from bodybuilding, he won another Mr. Olympia title. But his real goal was to pump up for his next movie role.

6

A RISING STAR

Most of Schwarzenegger's movies had played up his superior muscular build. His next role was no different. He took the part of a larger-than-life comic book hero in *Conan the Barbarian*.

Schwarzenegger was in good shape, but he needed to add to his massive muscles for the part of Conan. As an incentive to train harder, he decided to briefly come out of retirement to enter the Mr. Olympia competition. George Butler, who had filmed *Pumping Iron*, captured Schwarzenegger's return to competition in the documentary *Comeback*.

Even if his body had lost some of his luster, Schwarzenegger's cunning tactics were still intact. He arrived in Sydney, Australia, claiming to be there only as a television commentator. It was not until the day before the contest that he announced that he had actually come to compete. The other contestants protested his late entry, but they did not really think he had much of a chance of winning. Schwarzenegger was not in the same shape he had been when he retired five years earlier.

During the posing, Schwarzenegger told defending champion Frank Zane a joke. Zane burst out laughing and lost points. Schwarzenegger was awarded his seventh Mr. Olympia title. The crowd went wild, but not in the way Schwarzenegger had expected. "The audience was furious, throwing things, swearing. A great chorus of 'Rigged, rigged, rigged' flared up. There's never been anything like it in any bodybuilding contest ever. Everyone in the place was booing Arnold, shouting and brawling in disgust. Arnold was enraged and went red in the face."[1]

Reg Park was one of the judges and defended their decision. "There's a certain amount of 'presence' on stage which counts. Arnold had that appeal even five years after retiring. He wasn't the Arnold of '75, but to my mind he was good enough to win."[2]

After the contest, Schwarzenegger threw his energy into filming *Conan the Barbarian*. Schwarzenegger's character, Conan, has several violent, bloody adventures as he pursues his quest to get revenge for the brutal murder of his parents when he was a child. The movie was not well received by reviewers, but the audiences loved it. The movie gained Schwarzenegger devoted fans around the world and turned him into a global superstar. Conan earned over $100 million and became one of 1982's top summer hits. Its sequel, *Conan the Destroyer*, earned another $100 million when it was released two years later.

Inspired by *Conan*'s success, Universal Studio's theme park spent $3.75 million to add "The Adventures of Conan" to its studio tour. Audiences experiencing Universal's "Sword-and-Sorcery Spectacular" found themselves in the midst of a battle being waged with lasers, pyrotechnic special effects, and an eighteen-foot-tall, fire-breathing dragon. "The Adventures of Conan" opened in 1983 and entertained visitors for ten years.

Schwarzenegger's fame as an action hero was growing, but there was one title he had not yet achieved. On September 16, 1983, he took his oath to become a citizen of the United States. "I always

Conan in Pain

Producers often protect their valuable stars by using stunt doubles to perform the most dangerous actions. Although Schwarzenegger used stunt doubles for some scenes, he did many of the stunts himself—sometimes with painful results. On the first day of filming *Conan the Barbarian*, Schwarzenegger was attacked by wolves. He fell from a high rock and needed stitches to close the deep cuts on his back. More injuries followed. "I tore a ligament falling off a horse. I had my neck sliced by an ax handle. I jumped into a lake and smashed my head open on a rock. I was thrown off a camel," said Schwarzenegger.[3]

Schwarzenegger's injuries did not receive much sympathy from director John Milius. "Pain is momentary, film is eternal," Milius said.[4]

believed in shooting for the top, and becoming an American is like becoming a member of the winning team," he told reporters after the ceremony.[5]

Although Schwarzenegger was proud to be an American, he did not want to give up his ties to his homeland. His friend Alfred Gerstl pulled some strings, allowing Schwarzenegger to also keep his Austrian citizenship.

Up until now, Schwarzenegger had always played the good guy in his movies. His next film, a futuristic thriller called *Terminator*, changed that. He turned down the part of the human hero and chose to become an inhuman killing machine sent back in time to kill the mother of a rebel leader before the rebel was born. It proved to be a smart decision. Schwarzenegger's character spoke only seventeen lines, including the zinger "I'll be back!" Still, his movements and icy facial expressions were enough to terrify audiences.

"Becoming an American is like becoming a member of the winning team."

Terminator was a huge success at the box office and made Schwarzenegger one of America's leading male action-film stars. *Time* magazine called *Terminator* one of the ten best films of the year. Based on Schwarzenegger's strong performance, the National Association of Theatre Owners (NATO) named him the International Star of 1984.

Schwarzenegger was proud to be photographed with both his girlfriend Maria Shriver and his brand-new certificate of U.S. citizenship.

Unfortunately, success in one movie does not guarantee success in the next. Schwarzenegger's triumph with *Terminator* was followed by a box office bomb called *Red Sonja*. The movie was much like *Conan the Barbarian*, only this time it featured a female gladiator played by twenty-one-year-old Danish model Brigitte Nielsen.

Red Sonja opened in 1985 but closed quickly. The

Playing *Conan the Barbarian* began Schwarzenegger's rise into popularity as an action-adventure hero.

critics were not the only ones to slam the movie. Even Schwarzenegger thought it was bad. "It was a pitiful performance, and I was so happy that it did as bad as it did because people had no chance to see the movie."[6]

Schwarzenegger began filming his next movie, *Commando*, in 1985. It was another action-adventure movie, with the usual focus on explosions and bloodshed. Schwarzenegger's character killed off more than one hundred of his enemies, using a variety of violent actions. He blew them up, cut off their arms, and even dropped them off cliffs.

As in his other films, Schwarzenegger did many of his own stunts in *Commando*. Doing fight scenes and jumping out windows were nothing compared to his most dangerous stunt. In one scene, Schwarzenegger's character had to get off a plane during takeoff. Schwarzenegger had to hang on to the landing gear of the airplane while it was speeding down the runway at sixty-five miles an hour. One slip of the foot and he could have been crushed by the wheel.

Commando was popular at the box office and further cemented Schwarzenegger's reputation as a leading action-adventure star.

By now, Schwarzenegger was nearly thirty-eight years old. He had accomplished most of his goals. He had become a world-class bodybuilder. He had achieved success in films and in businesses. He was the author of several books on bodybuilding. But Jim Lorimer saw something missing in his friend's life.

"It's essential that you experience all of life's processes. One of the great, great pleasures is parenthood, marriage, grandchildren," Lorimer told him. "It's time you thought about marrying [Maria]."[7]

Schwarzenegger took Lorimer's advice to heart. Two months later, Schwarzenegger and Shriver were in Austria. On his thirty-eighth birthday, Schwarzenegger took Shriver out in a rowboat on the beautiful Thalersee, the lake in his hometown of Thal. He proposed in the romantic setting, giving Shriver the ring he had been carrying around while waiting for the right moment. "Are you serious?" asked a surprised Shriver.[8] She quickly accepted the ring and his proposal.

"One of the great, great pleasures is parenthood, marriage, grandchildren."

Soon after becoming engaged, Shriver was offered a dream job of taking over as coanchor of *CBS Morning News*. There was only one problem. The job was in New York City. Shriver had been working in Los Angeles for the past two years and enjoyed being near Schwarzenegger. "It was the job I'd always wanted. But I had worked a long time at that relationship, and I had just finally gotten it where I wanted it, and all of a sudden, I was faced with moving 3,000 miles away and pursuing a very demanding job."[9]

With Schwarzenegger's support, Shriver accepted the job and moved to New York.

It was a hectic life for Shriver. On weekdays, she got up at 3 A.M. so she would be ready to go on the air at 7 A.M. On most Fridays, she flew to Los Angeles to spend the weekend with Schwarzenegger. During this time she was also planning their elaborate wedding.

With the prospect of having a wife and children in the future, Schwarzenegger purchased a home in the exclusive Pacific Palisades section of Los Angeles. The $5-million estate spread out over two acres. It was covered with terraced gardens and had a stream running through it. The home included seven bedrooms, along with a swimming pool, tennis court, and its own gym. Sylvester Stallone and his wife, Brigitte Nielsen, lived nearby.

Soon, Schwarzenegger would be taking on a new role with a new leading lady. This time the role was not in the movies. It was in his life.

Arnold Schwarzenegger and Maria Shriver were married in an elaborate ceremony in Hyannis, Massachusetts.

7

RRIAGE
MOVIES

uncheon
decorat-
Kennedy
rt. Along
s a 425-
even feet
layers of
a replica
ad served

's friends
om the
dheim, a
l to the
llowed to
for the
he was
he had
ar crimes
German
War II. At
rzenegger
to Kurt
med that
im of bad
gift to
was on
o lifesize

ing of April 26, 1986, a crowd
reporters, and curious onlook-
g in a roped-off area across the
is Xavier Catholic Church in
hey hoped to catch a glimpse of
n streaming into the small town
wo days. There were movie stars,
ion broadcasters, and body-
witness the marriage of Arnold
Shriver.
ed down the aisle on the arm of
-edged white satin dress with an
d of the hour-long service, the
to the music of Maria's bridal
mmerstein's *Sound of Music*.

Wedding Security

Security was tight for the wedding of Arnold Schwarzenegger and Maria Shriver. Police officers began patrolling the area around the wedding and reception sites several days before the wedding. Twenty extra security guards were hired by the Dunfey Hyannis Hotel to protect the guests staying there. Shriver's family even convinced the Provincetown-Boston Airline to lock up its computers the day before the wedding to keep the guest list from leaking out.

On the wedding day, all five hundred guests wore small gold buttons that allowed them inside the church. Reporters, photographers, and sightseers had to wait across the street. All aircraft were banned from cruising below two thousand feet of altitude within two miles of the Kennedy compound between 10 A.M. and 6 P.M. The added security allowed the couple to relax and enjoy their special day.

After the ceremony, a wedding was served in one of two elaborately ed tents that had been set up at the compound in nearby Hyannis Po with the gourmet luncheon wa pound wedding cake that stood high. It was made up of eight carrot and pound cake, and wa of the cake Shriver's parents h at their own wedding.

One of Schwarzenegge was noticeably absent f wedding. Austrian Kurt Wa former Secretary Genera United Nations, was not a enter the United State: wedding. At that time facing accusations tha been involved in Nazi v when he served as a officer during World the reception, Schw: made a special toas Waldheim and cla his friend was a vict press. Waldheim' the newlyweds display. It was t papier-mâché statues of Schwarzenegger and Shriver dressed in traditional Austrian clothing.

After their honeymoon, Schwarzenegger and Shriver began their marriage, still living on opposite sides of the country. "I'm a very independent person," Schwarzenegger explained. "I can be alone and I enjoy it when we're together. Sometimes Shriver and I don't spend enough time together and, at other times, too much. But we make it work. I don't see a problem there at all."[1]

Several weeks after the wedding, Schwarzenegger's next movie, *Raw Deal*, was released. He plays the part of a former FBI agent who must infiltrate Chicago's most powerful mob family and destroy it. As with the other Schwarzenegger movies, this one is filled with blood and guts and a high body count. The movie grossed approximately $16 million at the box office, a disappointing figure for a Schwarzenegger film.

In addition to the time Schwarzenegger spent making movies, he and Jim Lorimer continued to promote the sport of bodybuilding. In 1986 they started a new competition, called Ms. International, to give the growing number of female bodybuilders a chance to compete at a higher level.

After the disappointing box office results from *Raw Deal*, Schwarzenegger was ready for another blockbuster. He got what he wanted with his next movie, *Predator*. Schwarzenegger played the role of an agent who went to

South America to hunt down and kill an invisible predator from outer space. The dangerous creature was in the form of a reptile and could skin a man alive with his thermal vision.

Filming *Predator* in a Mexican jungle was grueling. Schwarzenegger fell forty feet down a waterfall and had to swim in freezing water. To make matters worse, he was covered in mud for weeks. There were heat lamps on location to fight off the freezing temperatures, but they succeeded only in drying the mud. "The location was tough. Never on flat ground. Always on a hill. We stood all day long on a hill, one leg down, one leg up. It was terrible," Schwarzenegger said later.[2]

Schwarzenegger also had trouble with the huge reptilian alien, played by Kevin Peter Hall. The elaborate costume blocked some of Hall's vision. "Not only in the movie does he have heat-seeking eyes, but in reality [he] couldn't see. So when he's supposed to slap me around and stay far from my face, all of a sudden whap! There is this hand with claws on it!" Schwarzenegger said.[3]

Predator was a huge hit when it opened in theaters on June 12, 1987. It made $34.9 million in the first three weeks and stayed at the top of the box-office charts for more than a month. Schwarzenegger's performance won him the 1987 Male Star of the Year Award presented by the National Association of Theatre Owners. Schwarzenegger was also honored by having his star placed on Hollywood Boulevard.

The hugely popular *Predator* was followed by a futuristic thriller, *The Running Man.* Schwarzenegger played the part of a prisoner forced to be a contestant on a violent television game show. In spite of poor reviews, *Running Man* ended up as one of the biggest box-office draws of 1987. Schwarzenegger demonstrated once again

Schwarzenegger's performance won him the Male Star of the Year Award in 1987.

that he was worth the $3 million salary he was paid for the picture.

Schwarzenegger went from game show contestant to Russian policeman for his next film, *Red Heat.* Before filming started, he had to learn about Russia and the inner workings of the Soviet police system. He spent three months learning the Russian language, a job made more difficult by his Austrian accent. "It was not enough to learn English with a Russian accent; I had to learn it from scratch because the vocal sounds are quite different. Besides, the first twenty pages of the script are totally in Russian," Schwarzenegger said.[4]

Red Heat was a failure at the box office, but it still managed to make history. It marked the first time an American production company was allowed to film in Moscow's famous Red Square.

In spite of the film's failure, director Walter Hill was impressed with Schwarzenegger: "Arnold is a force of

Dressed in the uniform of a Soviet soldier, Schwarzenegger visited Moscow's Red Square during the filming of *Red Heat*.

nature. He was as friendly as Will Rogers, with a real sense of humor about himself, and he would go out there and fight in the snow with no clothes on and never complain."[5]

Schwarzenegger had proved over and over that as an action hero he could make profitable movies. Even in his most violent movies he had included humorous incidents and dialog. Now he was ready to take the next step and play a comic role. "Comedy comes naturally to me," said Schwarzenegger. "Even competing in sports, when everyone else was very intense, I'd always joke around. I look forward to doing straight comedy."[6]

In the movie *Twins*, a genetic experiment creates

a totally mismatched pair of brothers. Julius, played by giant-sized Schwarzenegger, is the perfect, innocent twin brother of mischievous Vincent, played by short, roly-poly Danny DeVito. The part gave Schwarzenegger a chance to show his sensitive side, something that had been missing from his action movies. He expressed real emotions, causing David Ansen of *Newsweek* magazine to comment, "For the first time since *Stay Hungry* he's recognizable as a member of our species."[7]

Ever since Schwarzenegger arrived in the United States, he had been a Republican. Even marrying into the powerful Democratic Kennedy family did not change that. He had backed Nixon and Reagan in their presidential campaigns, and he was ready to do what he could to get the first George Bush elected president.

"Comedy comes naturally to me."

A few days before the 1988 election, Jim Lorimer invited Schwarzenegger to come to a rally in Columbus, Ohio, to introduce Bush. When the rally was over, Bush invited Schwarzenegger to fly with him to three other cities. A friendship developed between the two men. Bush won the election and took office in January 1989. Schwarzenegger's campaigning earned him the nickname "Conan the Republican."

Schwarzenegger and Jim Lorimer had made great strides in elevating the sport of bodybuilding, but it was not enough for Schwarzenegger. He wanted to have a

After campaigning with George H. W. Bush, Schwarzenegger earned a new nickname: "Conan the Republican."

competition with his name attached to it. As a result, in March 1989, he hosted the first Schwarzenegger Classic in Columbus, Ohio. True to his word about increasing the prize money for bodybuilding, this tournament was the richest bodybuilding tournament to date.

Both Schwarzenegger and Shriver wanted children, so they were delighted when Shriver became pregnant in the spring of 1989. Schwarzenegger told Chantal Westerman of *Good Morning America* that he could not wait for the birth of his "Schwarzenshriver."

With her husband at her side, Shriver gave birth to Katherine Eunice Schwarzenegger on December 13, 1989. Having a baby was a big change for Schwarzenegger and Shriver. Instead of being two people with highly successful careers, they were now a family. Schwarzenegger loved being a father. He took an active role in caring for Katherine, taking his turns at feeding, burping, even diapering duties. He even put a cradle in his office. "I put it next to my desk and attached a rope that I would pull on. She fell asleep every time."[8]

"Becoming a father for the first time has definitely changed me, and for the better," he admitted. "A new baby is so helpless and so vulnerable and you feel protective and want to make sure it grows up the right way and is well loved and looked after."[9]

As Schwarzenegger took on the responsibility of giving his daughter a good start in life, he thought about other children who did not have her advantages. Using his powerful influence, he set out to improve the lives of children who were physically unfit, unsupervised, or mentally disabled.

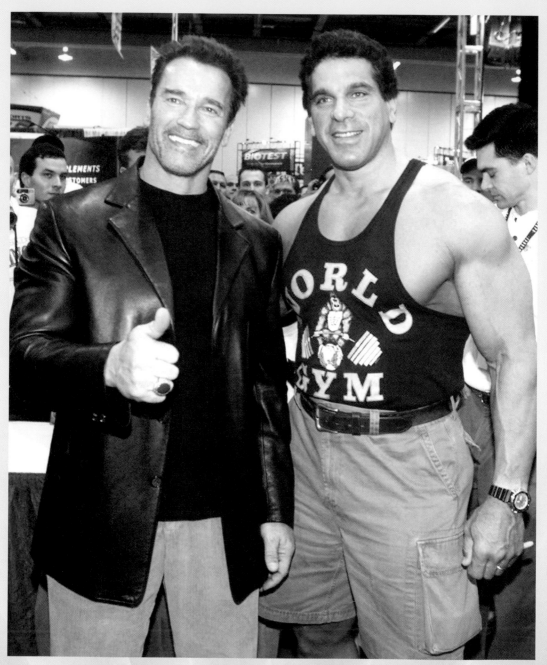

Schwarzenegger with Lou Ferrigno, right, at an event called the
Arnold Fitness Expo, which Schwarzenegger started as a way to
feature fitness events, competitions, and a demonstrations of
new fitness equipment.

8
PUMPING UP AMERICA

In early 1990, President George H. W. Bush named Schwarzenegger chairman of the President's Council on Physical Fitness and Sports. Schwarzenegger kicked off his national fitness campaign by holding the "Great American Workout" on the south lawn of the White House. Professional athletes and Olympic champions were on hand to promote their own sports and show that getting fit can be fun. Schwarzenegger had everyone, including the president of the United States, working up a sweat.

Schwarzenegger took his nonpaying job seriously. He traveled to all fifty states at his own expense and met with each of the governors to encourage them to support fitness in their schools. He also visited schools to get his message across to the children themselves. "It is just as important to grow up fit as it is to grow up smart. One without the other is not good," he told them.[1]

Schwarzenegger's life is full of contrasts. In his personal life, he promotes fitness and sets up programs designed to keep children safe after school. Yet most of his movies are filled with extreme violence. His next film, *Total Recall*, was no exception. It became the number-one film of the summer of 1990 and was given a special award for its spectacular visual effects.

In *Total Recall*, Schwarzenegger's character has a memory chip implanted in his brain, making him think he is a construction worker. He travels to the planet Mars to learn his true identity as a secret agent. When he discovers that his wife is a spy sent to kill him, he shoots her while delivering one of his catchy one-liners: "Consider that a divorce." Some were offended by the line, seeing it as a rallying cry for abusive husbands and boyfriends.

> **"It is just as important to grow up fit as it is to grow up smart."**

Schwarzenegger went from the violence of *Total Recall* to his second comedy, *Kindergarten Cop*. In this 1990 film, Schwarzenegger was a tough policeman working undercover as a kindergarten teacher to track down a dangerous drug dealer. He found that dealing with a classroom of thirty energetic youngsters was even more challenging than hunting for criminals. Although *Kindergarten Cop* did not earn as much as Schwarzenegger's action films, it brought in a respectable $85 million at the box office.

Schwarzenegger worked hard to promote physical fitness and to help with the Special Olympics. Another group that got his support had nothing to do with athletics.

The Simon Wiesenthal Center sponsors Museums of Tolerance in several cities around the world. It is named after Simon Wiesenthal, who survived the Holocaust, a program of exterminating Jews under the Nazi leadership of Adolf Hitler. When World War II was over, Wiesenthal collected information on Nazis to find those responsible for the millions of horrendous murders so they could be brought to trial. Their museums look at prejudice in the United States and the world, graphically showing museum visitors the horrors of the Holocaust.

During a special fundraiser that Schwarzenegger attended, Holocaust survivors displayed a quilt made from scraps of cloth from prisoners in

A Nazi Father

Schwarzenegger's interest in the Holocaust was personal. He had grown up in Austria, a country that had fought on the side of Germany during World War II. Schwarzenegger's own father had been a member of the Nazi Party. Arnold's views were the complete opposite of the Nazis' views, but his father's Nazi connection haunted him.

In 1990 Schwarzenegger asked the Simon Wiesenthal Center to investigate his father's war record. They found that Gustav Schwarzenegger had joined the Nazi Party on May 1, 1939, shortly after Austria was annexed by Germany. Moreover, Gustav had volunteered for the Sturmabteilung, or SA, the notorious Nazi stormtroopers, also known as brown shirts. However, by the time Schwarzenegger's father joined the brown shirts, their membership was declining. There was no record that he had ever been involved in war crimes.

The Simon Wiesenthal Center National Leadership Award was presented to Arnold Schwarzenegger by President George H. W. Bush in 1991.

the concentration camps. Seeing the quilt made Schwarzenegger wonder, "What happened to the people that wore that? Did they survive or did they perish? Those pieces of cloth—did it belong to a little child's trousers? Did it belong to a young woman or old woman? Or to a man, bereft because he couldn't save his family?"[2]

Schwarzenegger's own father had been a member of the Nazi Party during World War II, but Schwarzenegger had always hated what Hitler stood for.[3] He was generous in his support for the Wiesenthal Center, donating

$50,000 to the center every time he starred in a film. In 1991 he received the Simon Wiesenthal Center National Leadership Award.

Schwarzenegger helped out many groups, but his biggest concern was for children. As he visited inner-city schools to promote fitness he realized that many of the children had little or no supervision after school. They were exposed to the dangers of crime, violence, gangs, and drugs. "This has to change," Schwarzenegger said. "We can't let our children destroy their lives when all it takes is a few hours and a few adults who care enough to make a difference."[4]

During his school visits Schwarzenegger often asked the youngsters to raise their hands if they had television sets, refrigerators, and toilets that flushed. "Then you already have more than I did when I was growing up in Austria," Schwarzenegger told them. "I had none of these things, not even toys at Christmas. Now look where I am."[5]

In 1991 Schwarzenegger visited the Hollenbeck Youth Center in East Los Angeles. He was impressed with their program giving inner-city children a safe place to go after school. Schwarzenegger stopped by the center every few weeks to organize games, teach weight lifting, and visit with the children. He also gave the program a financial boost by donating more than a million dollars. He and Daniel Hernandez, the center's director, started an after-school sports program called the Inner-City

Schwarzenegger, chairman of the Inner-City Games Foundation, talks with children in a Chicago day-care center.

Games. The popular program reached more than one hundred thousand children between the ages of eight and eighteen who lived in the crime-ridden housing projects of Los Angeles.

The Inner-City Games were nine fun-filled days of sporting competitions. "It gave us a chance to go out and start programs to get kids away from those negative things and get them to do sports—and things like after-school programs, educational programs, computer programs and entrepreneurial programs," Schwarzenegger explained.[6]

The games were so successful in Los Angeles, that the Inner-City Games Foundation spread to fifteen cities. By 2002 more than two hundred thousand elementary- and middle-school students would be involved in after-school, weekend, and summer activities. According to Schwarzenegger, "Thanks to the games and their community partners, there have been huge changes in these neighborhoods. Juvenile crime and gang participation have been significantly reduced in many areas."[7]

Schwarzenegger was having more experiences with children in real life as well. On July 23, 1991, his second daughter, Christina Aurelia, was born.

Schwarzenegger had achieved some success with his comedies, but his action movies were still his trademark. His next movie was a sequel to the box office smash *Terminator*. In *Terminator 2: Judgment Day* (nicknamed *T2*) Schwarzenegger repeated his role as a futuristic killing machine, with one big difference. In the first *Terminator* he was a villain, but in *T2* he is the hero.

At a cost of more than $94 million, *Terminator 2* became the most expensive film in history up until that time. It was well worth the money. *T2* opened on July 3, 1991, and earned an incredible $70 million the first week. Before its run was over, *Terminator 2* had brought in more than $500 million worldwide, making it the biggest money-making film up to that time. At the Academy Awards ceremony, the movie received five Oscars for Best Editing, Best Sound, Best Sound-Effects Editing, Best Makeup, and Best Visual Effects.

Schwarzenegger and his costar Linda Hamilton were not nominated for Oscars.

Schwarzenegger used what he had learned in making movies to try his hand at directing. In 1992 he directed the Turner Network Television (TNT) remake of the holiday classic *Christmas in Connecticut.* It was his second time working behind the cameras. He had previously directed "The Switch," an episode of the series *Tales from the Crypt* that aired on HBO in 1990.

Off screen, Schwarzenegger found the perfect motor vehicle to fit his larger-than-life image. He saw a caravan of HumVee's being driven down a highway by National Guardsmen. Schwarzenegger took an

Schwarzenegger started a trend when he bought a military HumVee—which he nicknamed "Hummer"— for his personal use.

immediate interest in the military vehicle, which had been used in Operation Desert Storm in the 1991 Gulf War. He contacted the HumVee's maker to see if he could get one for himself. As a result, he became the first American civilian to own one and opened the market up to other civilians. Schwarzenegger called his new vehicle his "Hummer," and the name stuck.

It is not surprising that the Hummer attracted Schwarzenegger's attention. He had been interested in military vehicles all his life. As a boy, he often got rides to school in a tank with the American soldiers who were still occupying Austria after the war. "You might call it an armored car or even a troop carrier," Schwarzenegger explained. "Whatever you call it, it had a 40-millimeter cannon and it always picked me up."[8]

"I don't like the ordinary," Schwarzenegger explained when discussing his Hummer. "We all want to have a look that is our own. The whole thing is a game. It's all nonsense. This is the equivalent of a Harley-Davidson. It's that simple."[9]

While Schwarzenegger was cementing his status as a supersized box-office draw, he was also expanding his business interests. He opened his

"I don't like the ordinary."

first restaurant, Schatzi on Main, in Santa Monica, California, in February 1992. Schwarzenegger and Shriver designed the casual neighborhood café to be a fun place to eat. The food was mostly American, with some of Schwarzenegger's favorite Austrian dishes thrown in, including his mother's apple strudel. In a touch of Schwarzenegger's humor, German language lessons were piped in to the restrooms.

Later, along with other celebrities such as Sylvester Stallone, Bruce Willis, Demi Moore, and Whoopi Goldberg, Schwarzenegger became one of the investor/owners of several restaurants in the *Planet Hollywood* restaurant chain. The star-studded opening of each new restaurant took on the atmosphere of a Hollywood movie premiere. Each restaurant was filled with memorabilia from movies and television. Schwarzenegger's Harley-Davidson motorcycle from *Terminator 2*, the jet used in *True Lies*, the Alien from *Predator*, and even the tank he drove in the army in Austria—all found their way into a *Planet Hollywood* restaurant. The restaurant chain met with fantastic success at first and expanded quickly into other cities and countries. But several years later, after the newness wore off, the restaurants began losing money. Eventually, Schwarzenegger got out, taking with him stock worth about $200,000. That was much less than the estimated $10 million to $15 million the stock had been worth when he signed his five-year contract.[10]

Schwarzenegger's relentless energy allowed him to juggle his many interests—movies, business dealings, charitable works, and fitness. In 1993, he expanded the Arnold Classic in Columbus, Ohio, to a three-day fitness

celebration called the Arnold Fitness Weekend. He added the Arnold Fitness Expo, where companies could display equipment, clothing, and nutritional supplements. New events were added as well, including the Martial Arts Festival and a fitness competition called the Fitness International. There was also the Arnold Training Seminar, taught by Schwarzenegger himself.

To Schwarzenegger and Shriver, the Planet Hollywood restaurant chain seemed like a great investment—at first.

Giving fitness tips just to adults was not enough for Schwarzenegger. He wanted to get his message across to children, too. Since it was impossible to visit every school in the nation, he wrote three books of fitness advice for children from birth to age fourteen.

The success of Schwarzenegger's crowd-pleasing action films made him famous worldwide as one of Hollywood's top action stars. The National Association of Theatre Owners created a new award, naming him the International Star of the Decade.

The number of Schwarzenegger films continued to grow. *Terminator 2* had been a huge success, but his next movie, *Last Action Hero*, was a box office disappointment. In its first run, the story of a boy who finds a magic movie ticket that puts him inside the movie failed to earn back the $60 million Sony Pictures spent producing it. Schwarzenegger starred in the movie and was also the film's executive producer.

In spite of *Last Action Hero*'s disappointing showing, it made history. Columbia Pictures became America's first advertiser in outerspace by paying $500,000 to have the words "Last Action Hero" and "Schwarzenegger" painted on the rocket used in the world's first private commercial space mission.

Schwarzenegger and Shriver ended 1993 on a high note. In November, Shriver gave birth to their third child and first son, Patrick.

After the disappointment of *Last Action Hero*, Schwarzenegger needed a hit. He got it with his next movie, *True Lies*. Schwarzenegger's character played a top secret government agent who had his family convinced that he was a boring computer salesman. In order to save several American cities from being blown up by terrorists, Schwarzenegger's character did everything from chase a motorcycle through New York City on a policeman's horse, to reach out of a helicopter to pull his wife to safety before her driverless limo plunges off the bombed out bridge.

Schwarzenegger became the world's first pregnant man in his next comedy, *Junior*, released in 1994. His role confused his daughter Christina. "My youngest daughter asked me why I was pregnant now. 'Are we going to get a little brother? Mommy must be tired of having babies. Now Daddy has to have them,' she said.'"[11]

In spite of *Junior*'s mediocre earnings at the box office, Schwarzenegger was nominated for a Golden Globe award as best actor in a musical or comedy.

Schwarzenegger added to his long list of accomplishments when two more movies were released in 1996. He returned to his violent action-adventure format in *Eraser*, which did well at the box office. He finished the year with the comedy *Jingle All the Way*, which opened in time for the Christmas holidays.

Through his bodybuilding championships and action-hero characters, Schwarzenegger was known for his incredible muscles. The world would soon learn that there was a problem with his most important muscle of all—his heart.

9

GIVING BACK

Schwarzenegger's well-developed muscles and his emphasis on physical fitness made him seem like a perfect physical specimen. But hidden beneath his massive chest was a heart with a problem. Schwarzenegger had been born with a flaw in his aortic valve, the valve that keeps blood from flowing from one of the main arteries back into the heart. The defect had not given him any problems, even with his strenuous training as a body-builder or his physical exertion in his action films. Still, as Schwarzenegger neared his fiftieth birthday, he decided to have the problem taken care of. During open-heart surgery, the faulty valve was replaced with a valve from a human donor.

"Choosing to undergo open-heart surgery when I never felt sick was the hardest decision I've ever made,"

Schwarzenegger said. "I can now look forward to a long, healthy life."[1]

Some people claimed that Schwarzenegger's heart problem was caused by his use of steroids, but that was not the case. His doctors explained that the flaw was present at birth, and not related to the actor's early drug use.

Schwarzenegger's surgery was a complete success, so he was angry when the supermarket tabloid *Globe* called his heart "a ticking time bomb in his chest" and said that he was "living in fear that his heart will suddenly quit."[2]

Schwarzenegger sued *Globe* for $50 million in damages. When the suit was settled three years later, *Globe* was required to print an apology to Schwarzenegger and donate an undisclosed amount of money to the Inner-City Games Foundation.

After Schwarzenegger's surgery, his doctors told him to rest and avoid getting overly excited.

A Museum of His Own

Schwarzenegger got his start in bodybuilding in the Graz Athletic Union tucked into a corner of the city's soccer stadium. In 1997 Graz renamed its large modern stadium *Schwarzenegger Stadion*, a name it would hold until 2005.

Housed inside the stadium was the small Arnold Schwarzenegger Museum. As visitors entered the museum, they could watch a documentary of Schwarzenegger's life. The museum walls were covered with photographs of Graz's favorite son, showing his growth from a 150-pound teenager to a full-blown bodybuilding champion. The primitive weightlifting equipment he used in the 1950s was displayed, including the barbells he made himself at a metalworking shop. The museum closed in 2005.

Staying calm became impossible when a week after being released he was involved in a chase almost as frightening as a scene from his movies.

As celebrities, Schwarzenegger and Shriver were continually the target of overenthusiastic photographers, referred to as the paparazzi. Most of the time, the paparazzi were merely annoying, but one day they went much too far.

As Schwarzenegger and Shriver were driving their three-year-old son Patrick to preschool one day, two photographers working for a tabloid news agency called *Splash* began chasing them. Shriver, who was five months pregnant at the time, was driving. When she stopped their car at an intersection, one of the photographer's vehicles bumped hers. "I was terrified that he was either going to steal my child or open the door and my husband would try to hit him and have a heart attack," Shriver said.[3]

"My heart was pounding like crazy," Schwarzenegger later testified in court. "I was just trying to tell myself, 'Calm down, Arnold.'"[4] Both photographers were convicted and spent time in jail as a result of their behavior.

Schwarzenegger took a two-year break from making movies to give his heart time to heal completely, but he still managed to stay in the news. *Batman and Robin*, which had been filmed before the surgery, was released in 1997 with the usual amount of media blitz. In the movie, Schwarzenegger played Mr. Freeze, a giant human icicle

George Clooney, center, and Arnold Schwarzenegger at a publicity event promoting their new movie *Batman and Robin* in 1997.

armed with a weapon that could freeze anything or anybody that got in his way. It took six hours each day for the costume and makeup artists to transform Schwarzenegger into the silvery villain. Even though Schwarzenegger's part was small, he received $25 million for his effort.

On September 27, 1997, Schwarzenegger became a father for the fourth time. It took two months for Schwarzenegger and Shriver to decide on a name for their new son. They finally settled on Christopher Sargent Shriver Schwarzenegger in honor of Shriver's father.

Schwarzenegger ended his two-year break from movies with the 1999 film *End of Days*. The project had

Schwarzenegger's character battling Satan himself. After the movie was completed, a second ending had to be filmed when several priests objected to the orginial. *End of Days* failed to become a box office smash, grossing only $60 million in the United States.

The people of Graz, Austria, took pride in Schwarzenegger's success. In 1999 they presented him with their Ring of Honor in recognition of the pride he had brought to Graz. He was recognized for his humanitarian work in organizations such as the Special Olympics and the Inner-City Games.

In 2000 Schwarzenegger traveled to Beijing, China, to kick off the Arnold Schwarzenegger Film Festival to benefit the Special Olympics. The festival featured seven of Schwarzenegger's films, which were shown both in theaters and on television. Schwarzenegger was the first American star to be honored with a film festival in China. As part of the festivities, he also participated in the first-ever torch run at the Great Wall.

On October 28, 2000, Schwarzenegger introduced his next movie to the world at the 13th Tokyo International Film Festival. His newest sci-fi thriller, *The Sixth Day*, took on the controversial subject of cloning. Schwarzenegger played two parts in the movie—he is both the main character and the character's clone. When he and his clone were on the screen at the same time, Schwarzenegger filmed the scenes twice, once as each character. He had to act in front of a green screen and

imagine what the other character was doing. To keep in character as a cloned subject, Schwarzenegger arrived twice at the movie's premiere.

Schwarzenegger climbed the Great Wall of China to light the torch for the Special Olympics in 2000.

Schwarzenegger not only starred in *The Sixth Day*, he was one of the producers.

In 2001 Schwarzenegger received still another prestigious honor. During the International World Sports Awards he received their highest honor, the Lifetime Achievement Award. He was recognized for his accomplishments as an athlete and for promoting health, sports, and fitness among children.

The importance of these awards became trivial when compared to the tragic events that took place on

September 11, 2001. The world was stunned by terrorist attacks that killed thousands of people and destroyed the two towers of the World Trade Center in New York City. More people lost their lives as hijacked planes crashed into the Pentagon and a field in Pennsylvania. Schwarzenegger donated $1 million to the Twin Towers Fund to help the victims of the horrifying attack. Later, New York City mayor Giuliani appointed him to the board of a relief organization.

The September 11 attacks presented a problem for one of Schwarzenegger's movies. *Collateral Damage* was ready to be released and was already being advertised on billboards around New York City. A film dealing with a terrorist attack on American soil had a chilling similarity to the real-life attacks of September 11. With thousands of innocent lives lost that day, the studio postponed the film's opening for several months.

As he had done in China in 2000, Schwarzenegger visited South Africa to promote the Special Olympics. *The Special Olympics African Hope 2001* celebration had a historic beginning: Former South African president Nelson Mandela returned to the prison cell on Robben Island where he had been held as a political prisoner for twenty-seven years. Mandela lit the Special Olympics "Flame of Hope" for South Africa. It was a symbolic way of showing that hope and tolerance had returned to South Africa. After the torch was lit, Schwarzenegger led the Torch Run to Cape Town. The celebration also included an Arnold Schwarzenegger film festival to help raise money so that more Africans with mental disabilities could participate in Special Olympics.

For Schwarzenegger's next film, *Terminator 3: Rise of the Machines*, he came back as his most famous movie character after a wait of twelve years. Once again, the

The star of *Terminator 3: Rise of the Machines* poses with a cyborg model from the film.

Terminator returned through time to help save the world from destruction by machines.

Getting in shape for his *Terminator* role became more challenging than Schwarzenegger expected. His training had to be postponed for three months while he recovered from a motorcycle accident that broke six of his ribs. Even when healed, the fifty-four-year old actor had to avoid working out at his previous intensity due to his heart valve replacement in 1997. Still, by the time filming began in April, Schwarzenegger was muscular enough to make a convincing Terminator.

Terminator 3: Rise of the Machines opened on July 2, 2003, and brought in more than $44 million over the long Fourth of July weekend. Box office receipts more than covered Schwarzenegger's $30 million salary for his part in the picture.

Schwarzenegger's life was unfolding as planned. He had set out to be the best bodybuilder in the world. With hard work and determination he achieved his goal. Then he set out to make movies and became one of the most popular film stars in the world. He set the goal of becoming wealthy and used his intelligence and acute business sense to become a millionaire several times over. Now it was time to take on a new and even loftier challenge—politics.

10
THE
"GOVERNATOR"

Through the years, Schwarzenegger had stayed on the edge of political life. He had supported Republican politicians and served under both President George H. W. Bush and California governor Pete Wilson on their Physical Fitness Councils. Now in his mid-fifties, Schwarzenegger's appeal as an action hero was fading. He began to look at public office as his next career move. He was not ready to run for governor of California at the time of the 2002 election, but he was ready to take his first steps into the political arena. He did it through Proposition 49, a proposal that would provide after-school care to keep unsupervised children from drifting into trouble.

Schwarzenegger wrote Proposition 49 with the help of his political consultant George Gorton. His workers

collected 750,000 signatures on petitions, far more than
the 419,260 needed to get the proposition on the
Election Day ballot. Schwarzenegger donated $1 million
to help finance the operation. *The Los Angeles Times*
reported that both liberal and conservative groups "were
bowled over by Schwarzenegger's presentation of his
initiative, impressed by both his passion and command
of details."[1]

On November 5, 2002, when California voters went
to the polls, 59 percent of them approved Proposition
49, making the "After-School Education and Safety
Program Act of 2002" a reality. On a personal level,
Schwarzenegger had scored his first political victory.

As Schwarzenegger toured the country to promote
his latest movie, *Terminator 3*, Californians were
embroiled in a controversy over recalling their governor,
Gray Davis. Schwarzenegger was often asked in interviews if he was planning to run to replace the governor.
He avoided giving a definite answer until his appearance
on *The Tonight Show* with Jay Leno on August 7, just a
few days before the filing deadline. His announcement
that he was going to run for governor made such an
impact that *TV Guide* selected it as the greatest television
moment of 2003. After a colorful and sometimes controversial campaign, Schwarzenegger won the governorship
of the richest and most populous state in the union.

On November 17, 2003, Schwarzenegger stood
on the West Steps of the California State Capitol to take

Maria Shriver holds the Bible for her husband as he takes the oath of office as California's 38th governor. Supreme Court Chief Justice Ronald George administers the oath.

on the biggest challenge of his life. With their four children looking on, Maria Shriver held the Bible while her husband took the oath of office. After being sworn in, Schwarzenegger spoke to the seventy-five hundred invited guests.

"I did not seek this office to do things the way they've always been done," he said. "This election was not about replacing one man. It was not replacing one party. It was about changing the entire political climate of our state."[2]

With that, Governor Schwarzenegger rolled up his sleeves and began tackling California's problems. To prove that he was serious about cutting out needless

The proud family on inauguration day: The Schwarzenegger children—from left, Katherine, Christina, Patrick, and Christopher—look away as their parents kiss for the camera.

expenditures, he announced that he was turning down the $175,000-a-year salary that came with his new job.

Schwarzenegger's take-charge manner was apparent from his first full day in office. He quickly did away with the unpopular 300 percent increase in vehicle license fees that the Davis administration had put in place. Then he laid out his three-point plan to help the state's struggling economy. He proposed selling $15 billion in bonds to raise money to ease some of the state's staggering debts. He pushed for a constitutional amendment to limit runaway spending, and proposed a plan to tame the skyrocketing cost of workers' compensation insurance.

"This election was not about replacing one man. . . . It was about changing the entire political climate of our state."

As he had promised, Schwarzenegger quickly changed the political climate. Gone was Gray Davis, described as a "loner who had few, if any, friends in the Legislature."[3] In swooped Schwarzenegger, who made a special effort to build a relationship with leaders of both parties.

Schwarzenegger preferred to discuss politics in a relaxed manner over a good cigar, which went against the nonsmoking policy of his Capitol office. He got around the rules by putting a fancy smoking tent in the patio outside his office. The attractively furnished tent became a popular meeting place where the governor's

The Arnold Amendment

Schwarzenegger's political successes made some people compare him to Ronald Reagan. Both were Republican actors who were elected governor of California. Reagan went on to become president of the United States. Since the Constitution allows only natural-born citizens to become president, Austrian-born Schwarzenegger does not have that option.

Several bills have been introduced into Congress proposing a Constitutional amendment to allow foreign-born United States citizens to run for president. Not surprisingly, Schwarzenegger, who became a U.S. citizen in 1983, agrees with the change: "There are so many people in this country that are now from overseas, that are immigrants, that are doing such a terrific job with their work, bringing businesses here, that there's no reason why not."[4]

Others worry that an immigrant's judgment might be swayed on issues involving his native country or that the office of president could fall into the wrong hands. Amending the Constitution is difficult, and it is unlikely at this time that such an amendment would pass. Still, no one will say that the task is impossible.

visitors could chat, drink coffee, and puff on a cigar if they chose. It was a more casual setting than the formal governor's office. Antismoking groups protested, but the tent remained.

Once he was settled in, Schwarzenegger began working to set his policies in motion. At first, most California voters were not enthusiastic about Schwarzenegger's proposal to buy $15 million in bonds or change the Constitution to limit spending. But Schwarzenegger's heavy campaigning, along with endorsements from some of the state's leading Democrats, convinced them. Both proposals won by a large majority in the March 2, 2004, election.

Arnold Schwarzenegger received high marks for his first months as governor. "Unlike Davis, who was widely viewed as aloof, he is constantly in public view. And he is trying to both charm and intimidate the Democrats who control the state legislature," wrote *Washington Post* staff writer, Rene Sanchez.[5] Schwarzenegger made an effort to visit legislators in their offices, something that had not happened in the last four administrations. He sat down with individuals and small groups until all 120 legislators had met personally with the new governor.

In May 2004, the Field Poll gave Schwarzenegger a popularity rating of 65 percent, the highest percentage a California governor had achieved in forty-five years. Voters seemed to like Schwarzenegger's moderate approach to issues. He was conservative when finances were involved, but he was more liberal in the area of social policies. It did not hurt that Schwarzenegger's celebrity status gave him extra clout in pushing through the issues he believed in. However, his clout was not foolproof.

Schwarzenegger was irritated when the Democratic legislators failed to pass his $103 billion proposed budget in July 2004. He complained that the Democrats who refused to back him were too weak to stand up to special interest groups. "I call them girlie men," Schwarzenegger said borrowing a term made popular on the television comedy show *Saturday Night Live*. "They should get back to the table and they should finish the budget."[6]

Many of the annoyed Democratic legislators thought the term "girlie men" was an insult to women and gays. Rob Stutzman, Schwarzenegger's spokesman, tried to smooth things over. "It's his way of saying they're wimps, they're giving in to the special interests," he explained.[7]

Finally, at the end of July, Schwarzenegger signed the $105.3 billion state budget. It was a compromise that gave each party some of what they wanted. Critics thought Schwarzenegger's budget merely postponed the state's debt by borrowing from other funds to balance the budget. But the bottom line was that Schwarzenegger had survived his first budget. "I am pumped," he said. "I am ready to take on the next challenge, and there is no stopping us now because by working together everything is possible."[8]

Governor Arnold Schwarzenegger prepares a speech in his office.

Schwarzenegger's popularity was still high when he spoke to the Republican National Convention in July 2004 to support the reelection of George W. Bush. Before thousands in the audience and 30 million more watching on television,

"I am pumped. I am ready to take on the next challenge . . . because by working together everything is possible."

Schwarzenegger retold his story of coming to America as an immigrant and living the American dream. He praised President Bush for his leadership role and encouraged the nation to reelect him.

The governor did not spend much time campaigning in California for Bush. As expected, the heavily Democratic state voted for Bush's opponent, John Kerry. Schwarzenegger further distanced himself from Bush and from most conservative Republicans by backing an initiative to invest $3 billion in stem cell research.

During his first year as governor, Schwarzenegger had made many changes, but California was still struggling financially. In 2004, he laid out a three-step plan to address the state's problems. The first step would be to "stop the bleeding," or turn the economy around to keep the state from going into bankruptcy. The second step was to "heal the patient," or identify and reform the systems that caused California's problems in the first

Schwarzenegger promised to put his own muscles to work helping the first business that responded to his CALIFORNIA WANTS YOUR BUSINESS campaign.

place. The third step would be to rebuild California for the future.[9]

Schwarzenegger met with some success in the first step through spending cuts and encouraging new businesses to move to California. But his plan for reform put him on a collision course with the public-employee unions.

During Schwarzenegger's second State of the State address in January 2005, he outlined the sweeping changes he wanted to make to heal the state's financial crisis. Instead of raising taxes, his plan would balance the budget by making cuts in programs and services. He also suggested that for general expenses, the state use some money that was supposed to go for education and road building.

Schwarzenegger knew that his plan would be unpopular with a lot of people. "The special interests will run TV ads calling me cruel and heartless," he predicted. "They will organize protests out in front of the Capitol. They will try to say I don't understand the consequences of these decisions. Let me tell you something. I am well aware there are lives behind the numbers."[10]

Opposition was quick to surface. Millions of people in California were against various parts of Schwarzenegger's plan. By late June 2005, his approval rating had tumbled to 37 percent. Schwarzenegger, who a year earlier had prided himself on bringing everyone together, had now put himself at odds with millions of voters.

Schwarzenegger's prediction was correct. Millions were opposed to his plans to reform California's government. When he could not get the results he wanted from the legislature, he took the issues directly to the people by calling for a special election. Of the eight initiatives on the ballot, Schwarzenegger was pushing four of them. One would give the governor more power to cut state

Plenty of Californians expressed their anger at the governor's plan for the state budget, but controversy has never scared or stopped Schwarzenegger.

spending. Another would increase the number of years required for teachers to get permanent status. A third would have a few retired judges draw the boundaries of legislative districts instead of the lawmakers themselves. The last would keep unions from spending money for political activities without the approval of their members.

Schwarzenegger's approval ratings tumbled. He was no longer seen as the charming hero willing to work with Democrats and Republicans alike to reform the state. As he tried to win voters to his side, he ended up angering public employee unions including teachers, nurses, firefighters, and prison workers. The powerful unions spent millions of dollars in advertising to defeat his proposals. The attacks caused his approval rating to plunge to a record low.

Polls showed that even the election itself was unpopular. Many voters thought it was wasteful to spend $50 million on what they considered to be an unnecessary election when the state was already so deep in debt. There were also problems with Schwarzenegger himself. He made mistakes and often alienated the very people whose support he needed. "It's the arrogance that is doing him in," said Bob Mulholland, a Democratic political spokesman.[11]

While Schwarzenegger's approach "worked well in the recall," said Ken Khachigian, a longtime Republican strategist. "The problem is that it didn't wear very well over a period of time. After a while he was a governor, not an actor, and it's quite a different role."[12]

As expected, on November 8, 2005, voters rejected all eight proposals on the ballot. That night, Schwarzenegger spoke to his supporters. He did not concede defeat. Instead he delivered an upbeat message. "Tomorrow, we begin anew," he said. "I feel the same tonight as that night two years ago. You know with all my

> **"After a while he was a governor, not an actor, and it's quite a different role."**

heart, I want to do the right thing for the people of California."[13]

Schwarzenegger's political decisions have gathered criticism abroad as well. In December 2005, the governor denied requests for clemency for convicted murderer Stanley Tookie Williams. Once the leader of a powerful gang in Los Angeles, Williams had been convicted of four counts of murder and sentenced to execution. Capitol punishment is against the law in Austria, and many people there were outraged that Schwarzenegger would allow the execution. His decision was widely protested throughout Europe. Knowing this, Schwarzenegger quietly requested that his name be removed from the stadium in Graz. He wanted to avoid a media blitz over the issue of the stadium with his name by making the decision himself. He also said he would return the Ring of Honor given to him by Graz officials in 1999.

> **"You know with all my heart, I want to do the right thing for the people of California."**

Only time will tell whether or not Schwarzenegger will be able to win back his popularity before he runs for reelection at the end of his term. But as he has shown all his life, Schwarzenegger thrives on challenges. Gray Davis, who lost the governorship to Schwarzenegger in the recall election in 2003, knows firsthand Schwarzenegger's will to succeed.

"Anything is possible if you are willing to put in the work to do it," says Arnold Schwarzenegger.

"Anyone writing Arnold's political obituary is making a mistake," Davis had said before the special election. "Even if all his initiatives are voted down, he still will be a formidable force in 2006."[14]

As a young man, Schwarzenegger had a list of goals he wanted to accomplish. One-by-one he reached or exceeded every one of them. When asked how he wanted to be remembered, Schwarzenegger answered, "If my life is inspiring to people, that's a great thing. If I could have a footnote in some textbook it would be that I demonstrated that anything is possible if you are willing to put in the work to do it."[15]

No one knows what Arnold Schwarzenegger will accomplish with the rest of his life, but if his past successes are any indication, it will be something significant.

CHRONOLOGY

Arnold Alois Schwarzenegger is born in Graz, Austria, on July 30.	**1947**
Begins training at the Graz Athletic Union.	**1961**
Begins year of mandatory service in the Austrian army. Goes AWOL to win Jr. Mr. Europe.	**1965**
Moves to Munich, Germany, to train. Wins Mr. Europe, and Best Built Man of Europe.	**1966**
Becomes the youngest Mr. Universe in history. Buys a gym in Munich.	**1967**
After winning his second Mr. Universe title, comes to the United States and begins living in California.	**1968**
Wins Mr. Universe, Mr. World, and Mr. Olympia. Stars in his first movie, *Hercules in New York*.	**1970**
His brother, Meinhard, is killed in an automobile accident.	**1971**
His father dies of a stroke.	**1972**
Wins his sixth Mr. Olympia title and announces his retirement from bodybuilding competition.	**1975**
Wins a Golden Globe Award for the most promising newcomer for his role in *Stay Hungry*.	**1976**
Meets Maria Shriver. The movie *Pumping Iron* opens. Schwarzenegger publishes his first book.	**1977**
Graduates from the University of Wisconsin. Becomes a weight lifting coach for the Special Olympics.	**1979**

1983   Becomes a U.S. citizen.

1984   *Conan the Destroyer* and *Terminator* are released. Schwarzenegger is named International Star of 1984 by the National Association of Theatre Owners.

1986   Marries Maria Shriver on April 26.

1987   Honored with a star on Hollywood's Walk of Fame.

1989   First Arnold Schwarzenegger Classic Bodybuilding Tournament is held in Columbus, Ohio. Daughter Katherine is born.

1990   President George H. W. Bush names Schwarzenegger chairman of the President's Council on Physical Fitness & Sports. Helps establish the Inner-City Games Foundation.

1991   Daughter Christina is born. Is awarded the Leadership Award by the Simon Wiesenthal center.

1992   Opens his first restaurant in Santa Monica, California, and joins other stars to become part-owner of several Planet Hollywood restaurants.

1993   Named International Star of the Decade by the National Association of Theatre Owners. Son Patrick is born.

1997   Has surgery to repair a heart valve. Son Christopher is born.

1999   The City of Graz awards Schwarzenegger its Ring of Honor.

Makes a historic trip to China for Special Olympics; *The Sixth Day* opens the Tokyo Film Festival.	**2000**
Awarded the Lifetime Achievement Award at the International World Sports Awards. Goes to South Africa for the *Special Olympics African Hope 2001.*	**2001**
The After-School Education and Safety Act passes in California.	**2002**
Wins the recall election to become governor of California.	**2003**
Speaks to the Republican National Convention.	**2004**
Calls for a special election, but all his initiatives are rejected by voters.	**2005**

FILMOGRAPHY

Hercules in New York, 1970

The Long Goodbye, 1973

Stay Hungry, 1976

Pumping Iron, 1977

The Villain, 1979

The Jayne Mansfield Story, 1980

Conan the Barbarian, 1982

Conan the Destroyer, 1984

The Terminator, 1984

Commando, 1985

Red Sonja, 1985

Raw Deal, 1986

Predator, 1987

The Running Man, 1987

Red Heat, 1988

Twins, 1988

Total Recall, 1990

Kindergarten Cop, 1990

Terminator 2: Judgment Day, 1991

Last Action Hero, 1993

True Lies, 1994

Junior, 1994

Eraser, 1996

Jingle All the Way, 1996

Batman & Robin, 1997

End of Days, 1999

The Sixth Day, 2000

Dr. Dolittle 2, (voice) 2001

Collateral Damage, 2002

Terminator 3: Rise of the Machines, 2003

Around the World in 80 Days, (cameo) 2004

CHAPTER NOTES

Chapter 1. California's Crazy Election

1. Carla Marinucci and John Wildermuth, "Schwarzenegger Steals Recall Scene," *San Francisco Chronicle*, August 7, 2003.

2. Karen Tumulty and Terry McCarthy, "All That's Missing Is the Popcorn," *Time*, August 18, 2003, p. 22.

3. Adam Housley, Jane Roh, et. al., "Schwarzenegger to Run in California Recall Race," *FoxNews.com*, August 7, 2003, <http://www.foxnews.com/story/0,2933,93985,00.html>, (October 26, 2005).

4. Tumulty, p. 22.

5. Ibid., p. 22.

6. Housley.

7. Tumulty, p. 22.

8. Marinucci.

9. Ibid.

10. Michael Wallace, "Where the Golden State Still Shines," *BusinessWeek Online*, October 9, 2003, <http://www.businessweek.com/investor/content/oct2003/pi2003109_8863_pi031.htm>, (November 8, 2005).

11. Laurence Leamer, *Fantastic: The Life of Arnold Schwarzenegger* (New York: St. Martin's Press, 2005), p. 256.

12. Ibid., p. 282.

13. Lynn Elber, "Arnold's Marijuana Moment," CBS News, November 15, 2002, <http://www.cbsnews.com/stories/2002/11/15/entertainment/main529462.shtml>, (October 30, 2005).

14. "Crowley: Schwarzenegger's Apology 'Curious'." On the Scene. CNN.com.inside politics. October 2, 2003, <http://www. cnn.com/2003/ALLPOLITICS/10/02/otsc.arnold.statement/>, (October 30, 2005).

15. Charlie LeDuff, "For Schwarzenegger, the Last Piece of a Master Plan," *New York Times*, October 8, 2003.

16. Martin Kasindorf, "Wave of Anger Made an Action Star Governor," *USA Today*, October 8, 2003, p. 15a.

Chapter 2. Second Best

1. Arnold Schwarzenegger, "The Education of an American," transcript of speech from Sacramento Metro Chamber's "Perspectives" event, September 21, 2001, <http:// www. schwarzenegger.com/en/life/hiswords/ words_en_sac_perspectives. asp?sec=life&subsec=hiswords>, (October 30, 2005).

2. Nigel Andrews, *True Myths: The Life and Times of Arnold Schwarzenegger* (New York: Bloomsbury, 2003), p. 11.

3. Marian Christy, "Winning According to Schwarzenegger," *Boston Globe*, May 9, 1982.

4. Jerry Adler, et. al., "Building Arnold," *Newsweek*, August 18, 2003, p. 24.

5. Laurence Leamer, *Fantastic: The Life of Arnold Schwarzenegger* (New York: St. Martin's Press, 2005), p. 14.

6. Arnold Schwarzenegger and Kent Hall, *Arnold: The Education of a Bodybuilder* (New York: Simon & Schuster, 1977), p. 18.

7. Ibid., p. 15.

8. Wendy Leigh, *Arnold: An Unauthorized Biography* (Chicago: Congdon & Weed, 1990), p. 26.

9. Ibid., p. 26.

10. Arnold Schwarzenegger, "The Education of an American" speech, September 21, 2001.

11. Andrews, p. 26.

12. George Butler, *Arnold Schwarzenegger: A Portrait* (New York: Simon and Schuster, 1990), p. 31.

13. Schwarzenegger and Hall, p. 19.

14. Steve Sailer, "Commentary: A Unique Aspect of Arnold," United Press International (UPI), August 15, 2003, <http://www. upi.com/view.cfm?StoryID=20030811-101222-8174r>, (October 26, 2005).

15. *Arnold Schwarzenegger, Flex Appeal.* VHS Biography, Cat. No. AAE-14103, Paramont Pictures Corporation, 1996.

16. Schwarzenegger and Hall, p. 36.

17. Ibid., p. 37.

Chapter 3. Moving On

1. Arnold Schwarzenegger and Kent Hall, *Arnold: The Education of a Bodybuilder* (New York: Simon & Schuster, 1977), p 41.

2. Ibid., p. 47.

3. Ibid., p. 53.

4. George Butler, *Arnold Schwarzenegger: A Portrait* (New York: Simon and Schuster, 1990), pp. 21–22.

5. "Arnold Schwarzenegger," *Bodybuilding Universe*, <http://www.bodybuildinguniverse.com/arnold.htm>, (October 26, 2005).

6. Schwarzenegger and Hall, p. 52.

7. "Profiles of Arnold Schwarzenegger and Ralph Nader," CNN People in the News, August 22, 2004, <http://transcripts.cnn.com/TRANSCRIPTS/0408/22/pitn.00.html>, (October 30, 2005).

8. "Arnold Schwarzenegger," Bodybuilding Universe, <http://www.bodybuildinguniverse.com/arnold.htm>, (October 26, 2005).

9. Rick Wayne, *Muscle Wars* (New York: St. Martin's Press, 1985), p. 133.

10. René de Jong, "Up Close & Personal with Jim Lorimer!" February 4, 2001, <http://www.thearnoldfans.com/interviews/jimlorimer/jimlorimer.htm>, (October 31, 2005).

11. Arnold Schwarzenegger, with Bill Dobbins, *The New Encyclopedia of Modern Bodybuilding* (New York: Simon and Schuster, 1998), p. 695.

Chapter 4. Hercules Opens a Door

1. Nigel Andrews, *True Myths: The Life and Times of Arnold Schwarzenegger* (New York: Bloomsbury, 2003), p. 41.

2. Rick Wayne, *Muscle Wars* (New York: St. Martin's Press, 1985), p. 134.

3. "Arnold Schwarzenegger," *Newsmakers 1991,* Gale Research, 1991. Reprinted in *Biography Resource Center* (Farmington Hills, Mich.: The Gale Group, 2004). <http:// galenet.galegroup.com/servlet/BioRC>, (accessed through Infotrac, October 26, 2005).

4. Andrews, p. 164.

5. *Pumping Iron: The 25th Anniversary Special Edition*, Home Box Office, Inc, 2003 (DVD).

6. Todd Klein, "Arnold Schwarzenegger: More Than Muscles," *Saturday Evening Post*, March 1988, p. 40.

Chapter 5. New Challenges

1. Marian Christy, "Winning According to Schwarzenegger," *Boston Globe*, May 9, 1982.

2. George Butler, *Arnold Schwarzenegger: A Portrait* (New York: Simon and Schuster, 1990), p. 76.

3. Laurence Leamer, *Fantastic: The Life of Arnold Schwarzenegger* (New York: St. Martin's Press, 2005), p. 126.

4. Wendy Leigh, *Arnold: An Unauthorized Biography* (Chicago: Congdon & Weed, 1990), p. 160.

5. Ibid., p. 159.

6. Leamer, p. 123.

7. Arnold Schwarzenegger, *Flex Appeal*. VHS Biography, Cat. No. AAE-14103, Paramont Pictures Corporation, 1996.

8. Nigel Andrews, *True Myths: The Life and Times of Arnold Schwarzenegger* (New York: Bloomsbury, 2003), p. 79.

9. Marshall Fine, "The Villain," *Super70s.com*, <http:// www.super70s.com/Super70s/Movies/1979/villain.asp>, (October 26, 2005).

10. Leamer, p. 128.

Chapter 6. A Rising Star

1. Wendy Leigh, *Arnold: An Unauthorized Biography* (Chicago: Congdon & Weed, 1990), p. 184.

2. Nigel Andrews, *True Myths: The Life and Times of Arnold Schwarzenegger*. New York: Bloomsbury 2003, p. 97.

3. John L. Flynn, *The Films of Arnold Schwarzenegger* (New York: Carol Publishing Group, 1993), p. 48.

4. Laurence Leamer, *Fantastic: The Life of Arnold Schwarzenegger* (New York: St. Martin's Press, 2005), p. 143.

5. Leigh, p. 200.

6. Flynn, p. 85.

7. Andrews, p. 128.

8. Todd Klein, "Arnold Schwarzenegger: More Than Muscles," *Saturday Evening Post*, March 1988, p. 40.

9. "Maria Shriver," *Contemporary Newsmakers 1986*, Gale Research, 1987, (updated 4/27/04), (Accessed through Infotrac).

Chapter 7. Marriage and Movies

1. Wendy Leigh, *Arnold: An Unauthorized Biography* (Chicago: Congdon & Weed, 1990), p. 251.

2. John L. Flynn, *The Films of Arnold Schwarzenegger* (New York: Carol Publishing Group, 1993), p. 114.

3. Ibid., p. 116.

4. Ibid., p. 138.

5. Ibid., p. 140

6. Ibid.

7. "Twins (1988)," *Fortune City*, <http://members.fortunecity.com/andifritz/twins.htm>, (October 26, 2005).

8. Nigel Andrews, *True Myths: The Life and Times of Arnold Schwarzenegger* (New York: Bloomsbury, 2003), p. 239.

9. "Arnold Schwarzenegger." *Newsmakers 1991*, Issue Cumulation. Gale Research, 1991. Reprinted in *Biography Resource Center* (Farmington Hills, Mich.: The Gale Group. 2004), <http://galenet.galegroup.com/servlet/BioRC>, (accessed through Infotrac, October 26, 2005).

Chapter 8. Pumping Up America

1. Arnold Schwarzenegger, "A Secret Tragedy," *Newsweek*, May 21, 1990, p. 9.

2. Arnold Schwarzenegger, "Remarks at Sacramento Host Breakfast," Events Archive: Governor Schwarzenegger Speech Transcript: California Chamber of Commerce, May 4, 2004, <http://www.calchamber.com/index.cfm?navid=554>, (October 26, 2005).

3. Phil Hirschkorn, "Schwarzenegger Disputes Alleged Pro-Hitler quote," CNN.com, February 24, 2004, <http://www.cnn.com/2003/ALLPOLITICS/10/03/schwarzenegger.hitler/index.html>, (November 10, 2005),

4. Sheryl Berk, "He's Got Games," *InStyle*, September 2002, p. 567.

5. Ibid., p. 567.

6. Christina Valhouli, "Arnold Schwarzenegger," *Salon*, <http://dir.salon.com/people/conv/2001/01/29/schwarzenegger/ index.html>, (October 26, 2005).

7. Berk, p. 567.

8. George Butler, *Arnold Schwarzenegger: A Portrait* (New York: Simon and Schuster, 1990), p. 98.

9. B. Zehme and H. Ritts, "Mr. Big Shot," *Rolling Stone*, August 22, 1991, p. 38.

10. Laurence Leamer, *Fantastic: The Life of Arnold Schwarzenegger* (New York: St. Martin's Press, 2005), p. 251.

11. Mal Vincent, "Junior Gets Arnold in Touch with Feminine Side," *The Virginian-Pilot*, November 22, 1994, <http://scholar.lib. vt.edu/VA-news/VA-Pilot/issues/1994/ vp941122/11220056.htm>, (October 26, 2005).

Chapter 9. Giving Back

1. "Still Pumping," *People*, May 5, 1997, p. 96.

2. Ellen A. Kim, "Terminator Gets His Revenge," *Hollywood.com*, January 27, 2000, <http://www.hollywood. com/news/detail/article/311892>, (October 26, 2005).

3. "Snap Decision," *People*, February 16, 1998, p. 181.

4. Ibid.

Chapter 10. The "Governator"

1. Robert Kurson, "The Amazing Arnold," *Esquire*, July, 2003, p. 64.

2. Arnold Schwarzenegger, "Arnold's Swearing-in Remarks," Oak Productions, Inc., November 17th, 2003, <http://www. schwarzenegger.com/en/life/hiswords/ words_en_swearing_ in.asp?sec=life&subsec=hiswords>, (November 9, 2005).

3. Daniel Weintraub, "Schwarzenegger Blinked," *State Legislatures*, December 2004.

4. "Schwarzenegger: Let Foreign-Born Seek White House," *CNN.com,* February 22, 2004, <http://www.cnn.com/2004/ ALLPOLITICS/02/22/elec04.prez.schwarzenegger.ap/> (October 26, 2005).

5. Rene Sanchez, "Learning to Govern, Without a Script," *Washington Post*, December 11, 2003, p. A03.

6. John M. Broder, "Schwarzenegger Calls Budget Opponents 'Girlie Men,'" *New York Times*, July 19, 2004.

7. Ibid.

8. Ed Mendel, "Signing of Budget Big Victory for Governor," *San Diego Union-Tribune*, August 1, 2004, <http://www.signon-sandiego.com/uniontrib/20040801/news_1n1budget.html>, (October 26, 2005).

9. "Schwarzenegger Speaks," *The O'Reilly Factor*, Fox News, June 16, 2005, <http://www.foxnews.com/story/ 0,2933,159852,00.html>, (November 1, 2005).

10. Laurence Leamer, *Fantastic: The Life of Arnold Schwarzenegger* (New York: St. Martin's Press, 2005), p. 357.

11. Luiza Savage, "One-Term Terminator?" *Maclean's*, October 3, 2005, p. 28.

12. Peter Nicholas and Mark Z. Barabak, "Why His 'Sequel' Failed to Captivate," *Los Angeles Times online*, November 9, 2005, <http://www.latimes.com/news/local/la-me-analysis9nov09, 0,4880792.story?coll=la-home-headlines>, (November 9, 2005).

13. Michael R. Blood, "Calif. Rejects Schwarzenegger Initiative," *ABC News*, November 9, 2005, <http://abcnews. go.com/Politics/wireStory?id=1296195., (November 9, 2005).

14. "Gov. Could Still Make a Comeback, Davis Says," *Los Angeles Times Online*, October 30, 2005, <http://www.latimes. com/news/local/la-me-davis30oct30,1,3510164.story>, (October 30, 2005).

15. "Ask Arnold," *Schwarzenegger.com*, March/April 2000, <http://www.schwarzenegger.com/en/news/askarnold/news_askarnold_eng_legacy_442.asp?sec=news&subsec=askarnold>, (October 26, 2005).

FURTHER READING

Bial, Daniel. *Arnold Schwarzenegger: Man of Action.* New York: Franklin Watts, 1998.

Brandon, Karen. *Arnold Schwarzenegger.* San Diego, Calif.: Lucent Books, 2004.

Schwarzenegger, Arnold. *Arnold's Fitness for Kids Age 11–14.* New York: Doubleday, 1993.

Schwarzenegger, Arnold, and Kent Hall. *Arnold: The Education of a Bodybuilder.* New York: Simon & Schuster, 1977.

Sexton, Colleen A. *Arnold Schwarzenegger.* Minneapolis, Minn.: Lerner Publications, 2004.

INTERNET ADDRESSES

Schwarzenegger's official Web site, with up-to-date and historic information about him as athlete, actor, governor, and humanitarian.
<http://www.schwarzenegger.com>

The governor's Web site includes biographies of Schwarzenegger and Shriver as well as speeches and updates on the governor's activities.
<http://www.governor.ca.gov/state/govsite/ gov_homepage.jsp>

Current *New York Times* articles about Schwarzenegger.
<http://topics.nytimes.com/top/reference/timestopics/ people/s/arnold_schwarzenegger>

INDEX

Page numbers for photographs are in **boldface** type.